# The
# Fire Lily

# The Fire Lily

## A Life In Leadership Transformed

MARTIN THROWER

THE CHOIR PRESS

First published in the United Kingdom in 2023 by
The Choir Press

ISBN 978-1-78963-338-2

www.thefirelily.co.uk
email: admin@thefirelily.co.uk

Grateful thanks to

My wife Pauline – for her encouragement and support in so many ways

Cris Coe – illustrations and invaluable help at early editorial

Ashley Thrower – cover design

The many people who encouraged me to write

# Contents

# THE STORY OF THE FIRE LILY

The crackling flames rise skyward
As the waving grass is burned.
But from the fire of the veld
A great truth can be learned.
For the green and living hillside
Becomes a funeral pyre,
As all the grass across the veld
Is swallowed by the fire.
What yesterday was living,
Today is dead and still,
But soon a breathless miracle
Takes place upon the hill.
For, from, the blackened ruins
There arises life anew
And scarlet lilies lift their heads
Where once the veld grass grew.
So once again the mystery
Of life and death is wrought.
And mankind can find assurance
In this soul-inspiring thought,
That from a bed of ashes
The fire lilies grew,
And from the ashes of our lives
God resurrects us, too.

# Making Your Mind Up
## Sharing a life journey

Well, I've finally done it! This book is the result of ten years of people saying to me 'you really need to write a book'. Like most writers, this hasn't been an easy task and I had to get past a long period of saying 'Who will want to read the stuff I think I should write about?' It has taken a period of five years, but the time finally seemed to be right, following the most extended challenging period of my life. The unpacking of my mind has been therapeutic, demanding in mind and spirit, and often very emotional.

The book is the result of reflecting over the sixty years of my life, predominately with twenty years' experience of working in the horticultural business, and twenty years as an ordained priest. A large proportion of those years have been in leadership roles. I must not forget too, over thirty-five years of married life to Pauline! We both have a deep faith in God, begun at an early age, and especially tested in recent years. You will get to know much more about me as I share my life journey, which I have used to illustrate the subject matter in each chapter.

*The Story of the Fire Lily* (the poem on the previous page) I occasionally used to read at funerals that I was leading. It speaks of life that can be perceived as dead and gone, but actually through death is transformed into new and vibrant life. Whilst the story is appropriate at the time of our earthly death, it is also the reality of our daily lives. Despite making regularly a mess of things and finding ourselves in hopeless situations, God has the amazing ability to transform what seems dead and gone in our lives, into that which is new and vibrant. I believe that the way that this is executed is by each of us having the opportunity to combine what we call our own mind with that of the mind of Christ. Having the mind of Christ means sharing the plan, purpose, and perspective of God himself, to make a difference in the world. As the hymn writer Kate B Wilkinson opens with, 'May the mind of Christ my Saviour, live in me from day to day.' That

1

mind is ultimately the mind of God, a mind which we can access through the Spirit of God.

In my time I have read many books, papers, been on countless courses and conferences, on how to be a good leader, aspects of being a Christian, and more. They are very much the ideal, and there is nothing wrong with something to aim for. However, this book is much more about how it really is — up front, and as honest as I can be, protecting names and some personal situations.

Whilst I am sharing a great deal of my personal life, please remember that my reflections are very much my own and are offered for you to read, consider and reflect on too. I pray that what is written might connect in some way with your own life, maybe as a leader of some kind, or not, and leave you to make up your own mind on what is written and the challenges that are offered.

# Mastermind
## The mind of Christ

In writing about the mind of Christ we probably need to start with just reminding ourselves about Jesus Christ himself – who he was. Let's start with the obvious: he is the Son of God. Jesus is in existence long before his birth. The disciple John begins his Gospel with the well-known words so often used at Christmas carol services. He writes:

> In the beginning was the Word, and the Word was with God, and the Word was God. He was in the beginning with God.[1]

John writes his Gospel from a place of wisdom, knowledge and deep relationship with Jesus; hence we have this opening sentence which needs to be unpacked to make sense of what follows. There could be a great deal to write about here, but I'll try to be succinct. John uses 'the Word' to attempt to be understood by Jews and Greeks. Jews would understand it to mean God himself; the Greeks used it to mean both spoken word and unspoken word. If you use this crude paraphrase: 'In the beginning was Jesus, and Jesus was with God, and Jesus was God. Jesus was in the beginning with God', it hopefully begins to make sense. By using 'the Word', Jews would therefore consider Jesus to be God himself. The Greeks would connect Jesus with creation where God created all things by his word. He spoke and it came to be. So, this word is, in fact, Jesus, without whom nothing would exist. As John writes in the sentence which follows

> All things came into being through him, and without him not one thing came into being.[2]

God and Jesus are one. When Jesus is born, he is the human, physical, visual, perfect expression, manifestation of God who we cannot see. Jesus is the living, walking, talking God!

Jesus has many other 'names' throughout the Bible, some include: Son of God, Son of Man, Lamb of God, High Priest, Messiah, Lord. All of these describe aspects of his character; who he was, and is.

Part of Jesus' overarching work on earth is to tell humanity what God desires. His greatest desire is for people to know that he created them, loves them and invites them to be in a never-ending relationship with him. That relationship is spiritually empowered. Jesus knows that he has to die and prepares his disciples for that event, but tells them that they will not be alone, as after his death and resurrection God/Jesus will send the Holy Spirit. God comes as Spirit – not a new manifestation as we know that the Spirit hovers over the waters at the beginning of creation.[3] God makes himself known to his people as God (the Father), God the Son (Jesus) and God as Holy Spirit. Three manifestations of the one true God (A.K.A. the Trinity).

It is the Holy Spirit who ignites the relationship between humankind (you and me) and God in all his manifestations. It is my belief and experience that God's Spirit lives in every human being. At birth he put his breath (Spirit) into us. Not just in us, but also around us. There is no place that God's Spirit is not present. There may have been, or will be, a time in our life when we come to tangibly begin our relationship with God, but for us to get to that point, the Holy Spirit is already active in us, as well as all people and everything around us. We have, as Paul writing to the church in Colossae describes it as, '... *Christ in you, the hope of glory*'.[4] It is, as he says, a mystery. A good one, though!

There is more to come! Paul, writing in his first letter to the Church in Corinth, says that '... *we have the mind of Christ*'.[5] It is also written about when Paul and Timothy write to the people in Philippi, saying '*Let each of you look not to your own interests, but to the interests of others. Let the same mind be in you that was in Christ Jesus ...*'[6]

Another great mystery! If we were to stop and really explore what the possibilities are with this amazing truth that Christ lives in us and that we have his mind, the world would be a different place. We would be different people. Christ living in us is not to constantly point out how bad we think and act, or to tut-tut when his standards are dropped. It is more about how we come to know for ourselves God's love, grace, mercy and forgiveness. It is about how God continually renews our mind and heart, and how we can realign our lives to be more Christlike in a life partnership with him. It is an opportunity to see God the Father as Christ sees him. It is having an internal guidance system, helping us to explore the way forward. It is walking like Jesus walked, pursuing the goals he pursued, with his attitude and passion. The opportunity is immense. Jesus says:

> 'Very truly I tell you, the one who believes in me will also do the works that I do and, in fact, will do greater works than these, because I am going to the Father.'[7]

This is what God desires. A real, active and true partnership. Us and Him. Our knowledge and his knowledge combined. With infinite possibilities.

Rather than some understandings that suggest we are to copy Jesus' life and everything will be okay, God longs for us to get fully involved with him, through a relationship and being bold to be faithful to his work of transformation within us.

Dennis Kinlaw, in his book on the mind of Christ helps to summarise:

> 'To have the mind of Christ is to have his perspective, his attitude, his affections and priorities. The Bible calls us to have the mind of Christ within us, rather than merely learning how to imitate him. We are challenged to allow his mind to guide our lives.'[8]

Each of the following chapters will explore aspects of the mind that you and I (and particularly those in leadership roles) need to allow God to renew and transform, so that we might truly think, and subsequently act, with the mind of Christ.

# Tiny Little Mind
## Our mind and the brain

If we are to have the mind of Christ, how does that relate to *our* mind, and how does our mind relate to our brain? Therefore, it seems important to have some idea of how our mind and brain relate. I am not a doctor, which means that this short chapter is fairly basic (but hopefully in its simplicity still accurate!), so that we might have a foundation to explore further the desire to have the mind of Christ.

Israelmore Ayivor, an inspirational writer and someone who is passionate about leadership, says this:

> *'God calls big trees out of small seeds, so He prepares great monuments out of small minds. He will definitely call those wonderful things he put in you out of you. When He begins, do not resist!'*

Our mind can often be thought of as small. We have probably said or thought that someone is 'small-minded', or have had it said about us. What is actually being implied is that we may think in a small way. Perhaps we have narrow views and opinions because we refuse, or do not dare to explore wider ideas or see the 'bigger picture' about something. The mistake overall is to think that we have a small mind – it is absolutely not the case, for any of us.

Getting some overall idea of what our mind is, we need to have some understanding of our brain. It's crudely visually a bit like a rice pudding and made of 1.5kg of fatty cells. It is the most complex organ in the human body, being the main control centre for most of our bodily functions. The centre of who we are, what we feel and how we behave. Our mind is therefore an integral part of our brain. This is how our brain is made up:

1. The brain stem: the junction between the top of our spinal cord and the brain, comprises about 10 per cent of the central nervous system. It consists of three parts – first, the medulla oblongata, which is essential for breathing, digestion, heart rate and blood pressure. The second area is the pons (Latin for bridge) which assists in functions (as above) but also directs movement-related information between the cortex and the cerebellum. Then third, the midbrain, which is responsible for controlling and coordinating many of the body's sensory and motor functions such as eye movement.

2. The cerebellum (little brain) is connected and found behind the brain stem. It is primarily for movement and balance and receives and processes a range of inputs from the eyes, ears, balancing systems and cortex, sending instructions back through the brain stem to the other regions of the brain.

3. The diencephalon contains the thalamus and the hypothalamus. Thalamus processes and transfers much of our sensory information. The hypothalamus is connected to almost every part of the brain, being essential for motivation and seeking things which we find rewarding – such as sex, music, drugs, etc.

4. The basal ganglia, amygdala and hippocampus. The basal ganglia are vital in coordination of fine movement. The amygdala generates emotional response fear, desire and how we relate to the world around us. Hippocampus is where memories are forged if we are awake or asleep.

5. The cerebral cortex gives the brain most of its powers, providing us with the power of thought. It is divided into other areas: first, the frontal lobe – for attention, planning, language, movement; second, the parental lobe – which processes sensory information helping us to perceive the world around us; third, occipital lobes provide our vision; finally, temporal lobes for sound and language, memory formation and retrieval.

6. Corpus callosum is made up of a large bundle of nerve fibres where information is received and flows.

With this basic description of what the brain is, and does, we need to know that our mind is not the brain. However, our mind is what the brain does. It is, if you like, a communication and control system. It is our thoughts which are instrumental in changing our brain. The mind is basically in two parts:

1. The analytical mind – The rational, conscious, aware mind which thinks, observes data, remembers it and resolves problems.
2. The reactive mind – The portion of our mind which works on a totally stimulus-response basis. It is not under volitional control, and exerts force and the power of command over awareness, purposes, thoughts, body and actions.

Whilst humanity has tried to get to grips with an understanding of the mind, even in the twenty-first century, those who study this subject would still agree that the mind is so complex that to fully understand and describe it, and what it does, is a work still in progress, as are we, as human beings.

I believe that if we have the mind of Christ, it is about allowing God to transform those aspects of our analytical and reactive mind (above) so that we are a work in progress to become more Christlike in who we are and how we act.

# Don't Mind If I Do!
## Sacrificial servanthood

It was September 1993. I was watching the television. *Challenge Annika* was the programme, which I watched often. The purpose of the programme each time was to give Annika Rice, the presenter, a task to bring about a challenging project. She had to bring together people with skills and persuade companies to donate various items that were required. In this particular programme her challenge was to refurbish the crypt of St Martin-in-the-Fields Church, London so that the homeless in the area could be fed. As individuals were interviewed, I saw in the homeless the face of Christ. Tears welled up within me and I longed to be one of the volunteers to help the project come to fruition.

A few days after the television programme, I was at a prayer team meeting. I was part of a team of people who would regularly pray for individuals during or after acts of worship, and especially during services of healing. The person leading the meeting opened up, reading, 'Whoever compels you to go one mile, go with them two.'[9] The sentence stayed with me all night. Over and over again I repeated it.

The following day was harvest thanksgiving. Worship and sermon were based on Jesus feeding the five thousand[10] – a recurring story given to me throughout the last thirty years! Serving others and therefore serving God was in my mind, constantly. My journal at the time notes that I shared the above with others in the prayer team that I trusted and one responded with the message 'watch and wait'. There was also a picture shared of a vase with a gold rim, being poured out.

I felt compelled to respond. Talking through all of this with my parish priest, he suggested that I talk to someone and gave me a contact. Within a few days I was sharing with her all that had happened to me. She said that she saw the vase as me – beautiful in appearance and precious, but it was important that I was emptied. That evening I was listening to a song by a group called Nutshell. These lyrics jumped out at me:

*'My life's an empty page, O let your play begin … I'm nothing without you … An eagle without wings. If I forget about you, I lose everything …'*

And so, the journey to discern from God what all of this was about began.

During the last week of November 1993, my parish priest suggested that I take part in a week of guided prayer to begin the journey of discernment. If you have not heard of what that is (as I hadn't at that point), it is an opportunity to dedicate some quality time each day for prayer and reflection and meet with someone who is assigned as your prayer guide. Their role is to listen to what God may or may not be saying to you; suggest aspects or Bible readings for prayer and reflect back to you what they hear. Their role is not to counsel but to accompany you for the week. It was to be held at the local Catholic Church. This was a frightening challenge – first I was going on my own and second it was at the Catholic Church (talk about 'out of my comfort zone!') I share more about that time in the chapter about discernment – but that week was pivotal to my priestly calling.

The following two years, 1994 and 1995, became a defining time in my relationship with God. I accepted the invitation to take part in the Ignatian Spiritual Exercises.

The exercises were put together in 1522–1524 by Ignatius of Loyola. A Spanish priest and theologian, he was the founder of the Society of Jesus (Jesuits). Although designed to be undertaken over a period of four weeks during a retreat away from home, I undertook the exercises whilst working and going about my daily life. I met with my parish priest every week over almost a two-year period. The purpose of the exercises is to help individuals discern God's will in their lives, leading to a commitment to Jesus to follow him, whatever the cost.

My journal, at the beginning of the exercises, opens with this prayer by Ignatius:

> *Take, Lord, and receive all my liberty,*
> *my memory, my understanding,*
> *and my entire will,*
> *All I have and call my own.*
>
> *You have given all to me.*
> *To you, Lord, I return it.*
>
> *Everything is yours; do with it what you will.*
> *Give me only your love and your grace,*
> *that is enough for me.*

Whilst I remember praying this often, with all honesty and intent, I had no real idea of what God had in mind. In hindsight, it was clearly part of me (as the vase) being emptied.

During the two years of using the 'tool' of the Spiritual Exercises, I began to actively seek what God had in mind for my future. I spent some time with my spiritual director (see Chapter 12) reflecting on Mary, Jesus' mother-to-be as she is confronted by Gabriel, an angel, telling her that she is to conceive a son – not just a son, but the Son of God. After Gabriel informs her of how it will all happen, Mary seems to take no time in replying and says, 'Here am I, the servant of the Lord; let it be with me according to your word.' (Luke 1:38) Mary actively accepts and takes part in sacrificial servanthood. She is so focused on what is to happen that nothing else seems to matter. She doesn't say to the angel, 'let me just go away and think about that' or 'I need to chat with Joseph to see if he is okay with it all'! Her response is unconditional, trusting and with her whole being. I found myself saying 'yes' to God. The advantage that Mary had as she said 'yes' was that she knew (in essence) what she was saying yes to. I had no idea, except to know that God wanted my 'yes' in advance, perhaps to demonstrate my willingness to whatever, and whenever, he chose to reveal his calling. Perhaps another way of responding to God's calling could be to say 'Don't mind if I do'. I chose that response as the title to this chapter, not because it should be a flippant way to talk to God, but because of its most original use: 'Don't mind if I do' was a catchphrase popularised by Colonel Chinstrap, a character created by Jack Train, in the 1942 radio programme *It's That Man Again*. It means 'thank you very much, I am pleased to accept your kind offer.'

It was during 1994, as my parish priest encouraged me to explore priestly ministry, that I attended several different seminars. As I listened to someone speak about their ministry, a priestly ministry whilst continuing to work in the world of business, I felt a reassurance that I could not ignore. At the time, the Church of England called this Non-Stipendiary Ministry, using the acronym NSM. Because of keeping a full-time paid job there was no stipend offered – a stipend is not a salary but represents a payment to cover the costs of doing the task. Over the year, God led me to a place where I could use the words of Charles de Foucault. He was born into an aristocratic family in France. In his twenties he had a powerful religious experience and from then on, he dedicated his life to God. He lived among the people of the Sahara, and died at the hand of an assassin during an uprising against the French. He prayed:

> *Father, I abandon myself into Your hands;*
> *do with me what You will.*
> *Whatever You do I thank You.*
> *I am ready for all, I accept all.*
> *Let only Your Will be done in me,*
> *as in all Your creatures,*
> *I ask no more than this, my Lord.*
>
> *Into Your hands I commend my soul;*
> *I offer it to You, O Lord,*
> *with all the love of my heart,*
> *for I love You, my God, and so need to give myself,*
> *to surrender myself into Your hands,*
> *without reserve and with total confidence,*
> *for You are my Father.*
> *Amen.*

It is a prayer which needs to come with a government health warning! This is not a prayer to speak to God in 'a matter of fact' way. Using the words 'abandon' and 'surrender' are sacrificial. It is about giving the absolute all of ourselves, every single part, to God. It is a response out of knowing that God loves us unconditionally and we love him in return – with all of who we are, and will be.

Charles de Foucault echoes in his prayer the words of Jesus at His crucifixion (Luke 24:46). It is no coincidence. As Jesus hangs on the cross, he empties himself. The Greek word is *kenosis*, meaning the act of emptying all of ourselves so that we are completely receptive to the will of God. For me, as I said earlier, it was emptying the vase of myself. Paul, writing to the church in Philippi says this:

> **Let the same mind be in you that was in Christ Jesus,** who, though he was in the form of God, did not regard equality with God as something to be exploited, but emptied himself, taking the form of a slave, being born in human likeness.

> And being found in human form, he humbled himself and became obedient to the point of death even death on a cross.[11]

Being a leader with the mind of Christ is therefore about self-emptying and also about bearing our own cross. Putting our old 'self-focused' life on the cross so that we might be resurrected. This is not just a one-off event, but continual. We are all reminded by Jesus, who says: 'If any want to become my followers, let them deny themselves and take up their cross daily and follow me.'[12]

However, denying ourselves (self-denial) is not the same as self-neglect. It is a crucial thing to remember, and I know, out of personal experience, what happens if you treat them the same. God created us in his own image and loves us beyond telling. It means that we are important and beloved and our wellbeing is essential to ourselves and also to God. Elsewhere I will share more of my own experience when these two aspects merge and the devastation that can evolve, looking after ourselves by knowing that we are worthy to do so and not feeling guilty if we do. Time for ourselves to just 'be'; being conscious of our physical, mental and spiritual health and acting upon it; maintaining relationships and doing the things that we love and find pleasure from are absolutely essential. We are not going to be strong enough to deny ourselves for God if we are neglecting ourselves. We cannot effectively serve others if we don't serve ourselves. Living unselfishly, like Jesus, is a high calling and is grounded on love, and loving others in this way costs. You can't love others while you're staring into a mirror, or love and give to others while clinging to what you've got. Taking up our own cross, denying ourselves, makes others the priority. But remember, it is a critical balance between denying and not neglecting ourselves.

Whilst Pauline and I were staying with very good friends, who we have known for much of our married life, we had a discussion about a relatively new course which helps people explore the Christian faith. We watched together one of the session clips on DVD. This particular clip seemed to imply that when we become Christians then our problems become less and our life becomes easier with the knowledge that God is present. With the experience of priestly ministry and also as a senior manager and company director, I beg to differ! The reality of offering to God our absolute everything is extremely exhausting, tiring and risky. Jesus, speaking to Peter, says, *'From everyone who has been given much, much will be demanded; and from the one who has been entrusted with much, much more will be asked.'*[13] Our God is a demanding God. He expects, in fact he commands, us to love him and to love one another. There are many times when we will all fail to do that, but God is a god of intention. God is aware if our desire is to 'have a crack' at living out those commands, or if we just can't be bothered. If we desire to be faithful, then he is always gracious, loving and forgiving. There is that old saying attributed to Benjamin Franklin who said *'If you want something done, ask a busy person.'* As we respond to God's demand, so he keeps ramping it up! At least that is my own experience. People would ask me to do things because they had confidence that I could do it, and I would do the same to others. Those of us that get on and do things will keep being asked to do more. But remember the balance I spoke of earlier – at all cost.

I am possibly giving vibes that our demanding God is like some kind of driven, uncaring boss. That is absolutely not the case. When we are faithful to responding to God's demands, he is faithful in return, but often in triple fold to us. When we lived at Hadleigh, the deanery was a huge Victorian seven-bedroom mansion with a three-storey tower attached (the place where the first meeting took place to form the Oxford Movement[14]). With teenage and early twenties children we seemed to fill the house quite easily. We did have a spacious spare bedroom on the second floor and found ourselves taking in people who needed to use it. The first person who used it was a young homeless guy who enjoyed the occasional smoke of illegal stuff. Over a period of months before he moved in I, and others, listened to his life journey and situation to date. We had a spare room and he was sleeping in an old war shelter less than half a mile away from our house. It was time to practise what I preach and so he moved in. There were clear rules and boundaries, but a few of us spent time with him to begin getting his life on a better footing. We learned a great deal of how difficult it is to get help when you have no fixed address. When trying to get him a place to stay the authorities would not talk to him until they knew his address and had proof (such as a driving licence or bank statement). Totally bizarre when the point was that he needed help because he was homeless!

Our spare room was used by three others: a longer term stay with someone whose marriage failed, coping with accusations, and was suffering depression; someone who needed a place to start life again and get their family relationships sorted; and the son of good friends needing a place to take some time out before moving on. Taking people into our family house in this way was hugely costly. It demanded our unconditional love, counselling, listening ear and much more, on a twenty-four hour, seven days a week basis. Our children found it challenging (and occasionally so did Pauline and I). Having people in your private space takes a lot of getting used to, particularly in the early days until everyone is more comfortable knowing that they can be themselves. With the exception of one, our children managed amazingly to be open and accepting. Having the privilege of being part of people's lives at such vulnerable stages is powerful, particularly in the moments when you absolutely know that God is present and working through you and others to change lives.

Seeing lives changed is without doubt the 'reward' for self-denial. As people change in front of your eyes it also deepens our faith in God; he sees our wisdom and experience flourish and fuels our desire for God to continue his work through us. I have spent thousands of hours journeying with people as their spiritual director, parish priest and friend. Witnessing the pain of many teenagers being transformed into new beginnings and into accepting that God exists and loves them, and forgives them, will be etched in a beautiful way on my heart for as a long as I live.

During the peak of my mental health breakdown, I found a sermon by Dr Ralph F Wilson on servanthood. I want to share with you part of it:

*Jesus is the Master. We are the servants, some of us are head servants. We have been given responsibilities to fulfil in this age between Jesus' First Coming and his Second Coming.*

*Some have been given much and have produced much for our Lord. I think of the heroes of Church history... Some of these individuals were rich in the world's goods, but most came from poor homes. The riches they were given were spiritual, not material. I think of the David, the shepherd boy from Bethlehem, who, the Scripture declares, 'served God's purpose in his own generation.' (Acts 13:36)*

*I want to do that. I want to serve God's purpose in my own generation.*

*I want to be a faithful servant.*

*I want to be trustworthy among men, and trusted by my God.*

*But I have failed perfection. I have sinned. Yet I struggle to rise to my own expectations of myself and fulfil the dreams I believe God has put in my heart.*

*You, too, desire for God to use you. You have received much from the Master, and it is now in your hands to do with it what you can. To prepare for his coming.*

*You fall short. You, too, fail. But you do not quit. You do not give up.*
*Neither do you allow yourself to fall into self-indulgence and luxury.*
*Instead you seek His Kingdom and His righteousness. Your heart is on*
*the Lord, and he is leading you to do something important for him.*

*My dear fellow servants. I encourage you as I encourage myself with*
*the words of Christ:*

*Be dressed and ready for service.*
*Keep your lamps burning.*
*Be watching for him.*
*Even if he is delayed, don't fall asleep.*
*Be a faithful and wise manager.*
*Feed the servants under your care.*
*God has given you much.*
*Be worthy of that sacred trust he has in you.*

I don't think there is any other type of leadership that is not to be
sacrificial. That is if it is in the mind of Christ. It is high risk, often
misunderstood by others, sometimes repetitive and tiring, flexible and
variable, and the task never seems to be finished, and often we don't see
the results. But when God calls us to be 'head servants', he calls because
we are the best person, in the best place, to do what he requires for
whatever period of time, long or short. No one else will do. There is no
second-best option. God and his people lose out if we don't respond.

*O priest! Who art thou?*
*Thou art not from thyself, because thou art from nothing.*
*Thou art not to thine own self, because thou art a mediator to God.*
*Thou art not for thyself, because thou ought to live for God alone.*
*Thou art not of thyself, because thou are the servant of all.*
*Thou art not thyself, thou who art another Christ.*
*What therefore art thou? Nothing and everything,*
*O priest!*

Archbishop Fulton Sheen (1895–1979)

# Mind Games

## Good vs. evil

Before we get stuck into this chapter, let me lay down the basis for which I write. There is, no doubt, you would agree, a great deal of bad stuff which goes on in our world. There is also a great deal of good stuff too. My understanding and experience, is that God *is* good – the Bible tells us, for which here are two examples:

James writes *'Every good gift and every perfect gift is from above, and comes down from the Father of lights, with whom there is no variation or shadow of turning.'*[15]

Jesus said ... *'Why do you call me good? No one is good but One, that is, God ...'*[16]

I'm reminded of the song that is often sung with young people –

*God is good*
*We sing and shout it*
*God is good*
*We celebrate*
*God is good*
*No more we doubt it*
*God is good*
*We know it's true*

*And when I think*
*Of his love for me*
*My heart fills with praise*
*And I feel like dancing*
*For in his heart*
*There is room for me*
*And I run with arms opened wide*[17]

With great respect, it is a simple song because it speaks of a simple truth. God is good. I already acknowledge that you are saying to yourself 'but … but …' I know! But just bear with me.

If God is good, then where does that which is 'not good' come from?

Let's go back to the start and acknowledge what is written in the Bible, in the book of Genesis. You may receive this account as pure fact, or you may receive it as a story that tries to explain what happened early on in the creation of humankind using figurative language. In simple terms of my paraphrase of the first few chapters of Genesis – God, being good, creates the heavens and the earth. It is beautiful, with seas and rivers, trees and plants, animals, the sun providing light and heat, times of darkness and the seasons and various types of weather, and more besides. God is very pleased and moves on to create those who will care for his creation and also be in relationship with him and each other. Humankind (man and woman, we are told) come on the scene. Before God creates the woman, he commands the man (Adam) not to eat from the tree of the knowledge of good and evil, if he does, he will die. That is basically Genesis chapters 1 and 2.

In chapter 3 it starts to go 'pear shaped'[18], or should I say 'apple shaped'! Enter the serpent (a crawling animal or snake) who is *'more crafty than any other wild animal that the Lord God had made.'*[19] The serpent speaks to the man and woman and tempts them into eating from the tree that God commanded them not to. They fall for it[20]. The temptation is too great because they are desperate to be knowledgeable – to be wise. They don't believe that God will go through with what he said and they will die. The result is that they now have knowledge of good and evil but humankind is also to live a life which is cursed[21]. Good and evil now exist together in creation.

My own understanding about the serpent, the snake, is that it is not a speaking animal, but rather a figurative way of explaining the existence of the devil, Lucifer or Satan – three names out of many in scripture[22] for the one fallen angel who is also depicted as a great dragon in the Book of Revelation[23]. A fallen angel that is evil. The word Satan comes from the Hebrew verb *hitpa'el*, meaning to oppose, to harass someone – so Satan is the one who makes us trip and fall, the one who turns us from God. The word devil is derived from the Greek *diabolos* meaning accuser or slanderer. You get the drift!

Let's focus for a while on where this devil came from. If God has the character of loving especially his creation and the people he created and creates, why does he allow the devil to exist? The Bible and the tradition of the church understand and teach that the devil is a fallen angel. An angel who, with other angels, chose evil out of free will. Peter, in his second letter writes, *'For God did not spare the angels when they sinned, but cast them into hell and committed them to chains of deepest darkness to be kept until the judgement ...'*[24] And also Matthew in his Gospel records Jesus speaking about God's actions at the time of judgement *'Then he will say to those at his left hand, "You who are accursed, depart from me into the eternal fire prepared for the devil and his angels..."'*[25] The evil work of the devil and his angels is already defeated by the work of Jesus' death and resurrection, but we live in between that event and the event of Jesus return and the final judgement.

Living 'in between' is tough. It is a constant battle. A daily battle between good and evil. A battle which is played out in our mind, and the devil loves to play games with our mind, showing no respect for who or what we are – hence the title of this chapter. Leaders are by no means exempt from the mind games of good versus evil. In fact, I suggest, and experienced, that leaders are highly susceptible to such activity. The dictionary describes mind games as *a course of psychologically manipulative behaviour intended to discomfit another person or gain an advantage over them*. How fitting for the fallen angel.

Reading the story of Job's life affirms the fact the devil exists. Job's animals are carried off and a firestorm burns his sheep and servants. Raiders carried off his camels; a tornado destroys the house which his children were in and Job is afflicted by sores on his body. And there is more – as you read the book of Job. It all begins with the devil having a conversation with God:

GOD said to Satan, 'Have you noticed my friend Job? There's no one quite like him—honest and true to his word, totally devoted to God and hating evil.'

Satan retorted, 'So do you think Job does all that out of the sheer goodness of his heart? Why, no one ever had it so good! You pamper him like a pet, make sure nothing bad ever happens to him or his family or his possessions, bless everything he does—he can't lose! But what do you think would happen if you reached down and took away everything that is his? He'd curse you right to your face, that's what.'

GOD replied, 'We'll see. Go ahead—do what you want with all that is his. Just don't hurt him.' Then Satan left the presence of GOD.[26]

Although Satan initiates and causes tragedy around and to Job's life, it is important to see that God restrains his activity. God allows Satan to do whatever he wants with whatever is Job's, but he is not allowed to hurt Job. The restraining and controlling hand of God is in action. The result of Satan's work with Job is that Satan loses his bet! Job does not curse God because of what happens to him, but continues to be faithful and knows that God is good. Whilst God allows, with boundaries, for individuals to be tested and tempted by the work of the devil, it does not change the character of God, for he remains perfect and sinless. James, in his letter writes to remind the twelve tribes in the Dispersion[27], and us, saying that no one, when tempted, should say that it is God who is tempting because God cannot be tempted by evil and he tempts no one.[28]

The Catechism – the summary of beliefs in the Catholic Church (No. 395) states 'It is a great mystery that the providence should admit diabolical activity, but we know that in everything God works for good with those who love him.'

With all of this in mind, I find it staggering that so many people who profess to be Christian openly declare that they don't believe in the devil – and that includes, alarmingly, senior Christian leaders. Surely that is saying that they don't believe in sin? In which case, what was the point of Jesus birth, life and ministry, death and resurrection? I have even heard those who don't believe in the devil to be reciting Peter's words in his first letter 'Discipline yourselves; keep alert. Like a roaring lion your adversary the devil prowls around, looking for someone to devour. Resist him, steadfast in your faith ...'[29] Those words are used often in the Anglican Liturgy of Compline.[30] Since when did Jesus invite us into a Godly relationship that would mean everything is all nice and beautiful? I think not! In fact, I know not! Jesus tells his disciples '... take up your cross, and follow me.'[31]

Following 'my world falling apart', I understand that my churches were informed during the official Sunday briefing by a senior member of diocesan clergy that what I had done was not because of God and was not because of the devil. Need I say what theology was going on here? If what we do is not of God, and is not of evil (the devil etc.), then what is it, may I ask? Whilst there were many aspects underlying, my illegal actions were most definitely not becoming of the high office that I held and were certainly not Godly. Rowan Williams has something to say about this in his book Open to Judgement in chapter 17 headed 'An enemy hath done this.' He writes:

An enemy hath done this ... How can I be responsible for what I did not mean? ... it sounds painfully like the child's evasion of responsibility – the refusal to be adult and accept the consequences of our actions. But perhaps there is more to it – another kind of maturity which understands that 'responsibility' is not the last word about behaviour ... For human activity is misunderstood if it is seen as a sequence of 'responsible' decisions taken by a conscious and self-aware person, in control of his life ... More perhaps than we ever realise or accept with our minds, we are being acted upon as much as acting; and if our assumption of 'responsibility' rests on a belief that we can construct the patterns of our own lives, it is an illusion...

He continues:

It is not at all comforting to recognise that we are not 'in control', that incomprehensible forces are at work in and through us, involving us willy-nilly in a bewildering and horrifying chain of events.

22

It is absolutely right that as individual human beings we should take full responsibility for our actions. It is essential that we have some understanding of the complexities of what is going on mentally and spiritually in our minds that results in our actions.

Thomas Merton said:

> The devil is no fool. He can get people feeling about heaven the way they ought to feel about hell. He can make them fear the means of grace the way they do not fear sin. And he does so, not by light but by obscurity, not by realities but by shadows; not by clarity and substance, but by dreams and the creatures of psychosis. And men are so poor in intellect that a few cold chills down their spine will be enough to keep them from ever finding out the truth about anything.

He also said:

> The devil makes many disciples by preaching against sin. He convinces them that the great evil of sin, induces a crisis of guilt by which 'God is satisfied,' and after that he lets them spend the rest of their lives meditating on the intense sinfulness and evident reprobation of other men.

We need to get real. There are complex spiritual forces around and in us, and to ignore that reality is to allow evil to win whilst we carry on our lives in blissful ignorance that we live in the battle between the time of Jesus conquering sin and death, and the fulfilment of that event when it will be no more.

Thinking that good and evil is as clear as black and white is, I believe, not true and unhelpful. It is complex. So, if there is a 'grey area', how might we cope with that?

A key starting point is that we need to acknowledge that evil exists and as the people of God we are to battle against it. Our mind is therefore a battlefield and we need to know how to maintain the mind of Christ.

Paul, writing to the church in Ephesus, says to them:

> *For our struggle is not against enemies of blood and flesh, but against the rulers, against the authorities, against the cosmic powers of this present darkness, against the spiritual forces of evil in the heavenly places. Therefore, take up the whole armour of God, so that you may be able to withstand on that evil day, and having done everything, to stand firm.*[32]

He goes on to detail what the whole armour of God is. What Paul is saying, is that when we go into battle against evil, it is imperative that we go prepared and protected. That protection (armour) consists of declaring truth; knowing that we are 'right' with God (that we are righteousness); that we are at peace with him and ourselves; that we have faith in the God of goodness; that we know for ourselves the work of salvation that Jesus accomplished by his life, death and resurrection and that we proclaim the sword of the Spirit (which is speaking God's words). This powerful armour and how to use it is demonstrated as Jesus battles with Satan in the dessert.[33] Jesus stands firm and ultimately wins the battle.

We have authority to fight the battle. Luke tells us in his Gospel[34] that Jesus commissioned and sent out in pairs seventy disciples/apostles who were the first missionaries. Jesus tells them that they will be like lambs among wolves (or perhaps good among evil?) When they returned from their mission, Luke writes:

> *Then the seventy returned with joy, saying, 'Lord, even the demons are subject to us in Your name.'*

> *And He said to them, 'I saw Satan fall like lightning from heaven. Behold, I give you the authority to trample on serpents and scorpions, and over all the power of the enemy, and nothing shall by any means hurt you. Nevertheless, do not rejoice in this, that the spirits are subject to you, but rather rejoice because your names are written in heaven.'*[35]

Here is a truth: As leaders it is essential to be confident that Jesus has given us authority to trample over the power of the enemy. It is not your power, or my power, but the power of the crucified and risen Jesus that works in and through us.

Because the devil is 'the accuser', he will constantly mess with our mind, pointing out our flaws, suspicions, doubts, fears and tell us that we are not worthy. Don't listen. He is the father of lies! On those days when the 'little red guy' (the devil) sits on your shoulder and whispers in your ear and tries to mess with your mind, do what my spiritual director used to tell me to do – find a place to shout, 'In the name of Jesus p*ss off!!' I must admit – it works for me! Make a conscious effort to:

Live in the present, not the past or the future.

Be positive and surround and consult those who are positive people. Look for blessings – how and who is blessing you. Enjoy life in its fullness.

Stand firm. Be calm in adversity.

Be like Job – don't blame God with wrongdoing, or blame him for evil. We need to trust him through the mysterious circumstances of our lives. I know that's easier said than done.

God uses Satan's schemes to strengthen us. That was certainly the case when Jesus is in the wilderness being tempted. These times are life and relationship testing and training, not punishment for what we might have done. My experience, as with Job, is that God never allows or gives us that with which we cannot cope, for he is present and active in the tough stuff – the suffering and the battle. We are to reveal the character of God through our circumstances. James writes a truth, which is incredibly difficult and challenging, but nevertheless a reality:

*Consider it a sheer gift, friends, when tests and challenges come at you from all sides. You know that under pressure, your faith-life is forced into the open and shows its true colours. So, don't try to get out of anything prematurely. Let it do its work so you become mature and well-developed, not deficient in any way.* [36]

The reality is that we will screw up. Maybe it's because of sin; we make bad choices; we ignore God and proclaim he can't possibly exist because we are having a tough time, and probably much more. We then realise that we must have 'blown it' with God. We think that the direction we have started to travel has destroyed what God desires for us and it is not redeemable. But we couldn't be any further from the truth. Someone I believed to be a friend at the time and was most certainly used by God, sent me these words in a picture frame.

*If you think you've blown God's plan for your life, rest in this. You, my beautiful friend, are not that powerful.* [37]

Awesome, or what?! God loves us beyond all measure and there is absolutely nothing that we can do that will destroy what he desires for us. We are, and have been redeemed. In other words, God, by Jesus's death on the cross, has already paid the cost of our wrongdoings.

There can be, and is, I believe, a great danger that we can spend too much time and energy, spiritual and mental, focusing on sin and evil. I am sure that is to the delight of the devil. Doing what I suspect we all do too much, is to beat ourselves up about how sinful and useless we are, how worthless we feel and how things are so bad for us and around us. My wife, Pauline, attended a church service where the leader started the service with a prayer – nothing wrong there! However, in a deep and over sincere manner he reminded everyone, and indeed God too, that we were not worthy people because of our sin. Absolute rot! You, I and the whole of the people God created and creates ARE worthy, valued and loved. It is without measure. We do fall, we do make mistakes, sometimes serious ones and lean on the side of evil BUT we ARE loved beyond all of that for eternity.

It is during the times that we are battling against evil, battling against the tough circumstances we find ourselves in, it is essential that we beat that battle by turning our attention on 'good'. During the 'Job period', when my sin was public and I was mentally unwell and the future was at risk and unknown, my relationship with Pauline was secure and we were challenged to see that what was going on was blessing. That seemed crazy – to experience your life being publicly judged and your 'world seemingly falling apart', to focus on the blessings. In other words, to focus on what was good. It makes sense, because if God is good, then that which is good in our lives is of God. So, where was God in all of this? We decided to get out of the cupboard a book of large, clean white paper. Each day Pauline and I reflected on the previous day and wrote down what was good and positive. We used coloured (and sometime sparkly!) ink pens to be a physical symbol of happiness, thankfulness and rejoicing. Without exception, every day for ten months, there was ALWAYS at least one thing written down. Sometimes more, many more. God was in the tough circumstances, the trauma, and the dark days and was making it abundantly clear that good was battling against evil. That light was in the darkness in a real, powerful and measurable way. We have still kept the seventeen A3-sized sheets of paper. They will always be a symbol of God overcoming the mind games that evil tries to play. I am reminded of the words of that 'old hymn':

> When upon life's billows you are tempest tossed,
> When you are discouraged, thinking all is lost,
> Count your many blessings, name them one by one,
> And it will surprise you what the Lord hath done.
>
> Count your blessings, name them one by one,
> Count your blessings, see what God hath done!
> Count your blessings, name them one by one,
> And it will surprise you what the Lord hath done.
>
> Are you ever burdened with a load of care?
> Does the cross seem heavy you are called to bear?
> Count your many blessings, every doubt will fly,
> And you will keep singing as the days go by.

*When you look at others with their lands and gold,*
*Think that Christ has promised you His wealth untold;*
*Count your many blessings. Wealth can never buy*
*Your reward in heaven, nor your home on high.*

*So, amid the conflict whether great or small,*
*Do not be disheartened, God is over all;*
*Count your many blessings, angels will attend,*
*Help and comfort give you to your journey's end.[38]*

In those challenging days when God may seem distant and life is difficult to live, there are tools which we can use. Picking up a Bible and turning to your favourite reading/s, particularly those which speak about God's goodness, the work of Jesus, etc. Playing your favourite hymn/song. Reading your journal (if you have one). Looking at art and creation and reflecting on God's character. However, sometimes this is easier said than done. Sometimes the battle is intense and wanting to focus on God is impossible, in which case, sharing the situation with a close friend who will listen and pray for you is really important, so that you don't feel alone and know that someone is supporting you.

When we consider the work of evil, there is a danger that anything and everything that happens which is not 'good' is the work of the devil. It is not always as simple as that to categorise. As I have said before, it is complex. Just because something is not what we might call 'good' for us, doesn't mean that God wants it to happen and that he is instrumental in it. Discernment is therefore key to determining what might be going on (see the chapter headed 'Great minds think alike'). Being cautious is essential when it comes to talking about demons and particularly that someone may be demonic. Very often someone's behaviour is because of mental illness and there are plenty of scary and horrific stories of seemingly well-intended Christians praying outrageously over someone in an attempt to cast out demons. The Deliverance Ministry (ministering to someone or situation to deliver them from the devil) must come with great caution. Some churches have very clear guidelines and my experience of the Church of England is that this ministry is carried out by wise and experienced priests. It is certainly not a ministry to be carried out on your own. Over many years I ministered as part of a team of people and we would always work together in teams of at least two or more. I am not intending to share a great deal about this subject, simply to say that I have encountered people who say that people are not demonic. My experience is that occasionally there are such people. I have seen and been involved in such a case. When our drop-in youth club operated on a Friday night, we would always have a small team of people praying whilst it was going on. I believed it essential as many of the young people had deep issues they were dealing with and many serious behavioural problems. One evening a troubled young man arrived at the church door with a four-pack of lager beer. We took him into the prayer room to explain that alcohol was not allowed on site. He kicked-off in a spectacular way, shouting and swearing and then began to shake. His eyes turned orange-red and then a look of horror on his face. He spat at my youth worker a few times when he held him down. A couple of the prayer team were laying their hands on his back whilst praying and I made every attempt to stare into his eyes. We prayed with confidence in the name of Jesus Christ that all that was evil would leave. It was a struggle and I have no idea how long it was before the situation changed – but it did! He became calm and a long conversation followed. On leaving, he left the alcohol behind, saying that he was giving up drinking. He kept to his word for months and for all I know, years. He ended up being in social media contact with a member of our family, and would recall with them what had happened and the conversation he had afterwards with me. He moved to London and was keen to share his belief in God and that he had joined a young and exciting church. Such events are not often, but they are real, and unquestionably true.

I have also been involved often in blessing people's homes and businesses. Praying that anything ungodly would be sent out. Just flicking some holy water around or waving a cross is only a symbol of what is going on. The key to such ministry is praying out loud in the name of Jesus Christ. It is his authority, and his alone that is in play and it is a privilege that God may choose any one of us to work that ministry through. I never went to such situations alone, always with one other person who had experience, and also asking two people to pray at home whilst we were there. So often, people said how different the place felt and that it had a spiritual impact on those who went on to live or work in that space. Praise God, who has the victory.

We must always remember that God has won the victory over evil. The Catholic Church and some 'wings' of the Anglican Church keep the Feast Day of Michael and All Angels which is on 29 September.

During my sabbatical placement at Coventry Cathedral, I saw close up the bronze sculpture that is displayed on the south end of the east wall outside of the new Cathedral of St Michael. The 1958 bronze sculpture by Jacob Epstein, depicts St Michael slaying the devil.

The sculpture symbolises the victory of good over evil, and depicts a winged angel with spear, standing with arms and legs spread above the bound figure of the horned devil lying supine.

Michael is mentioned three times in the Old Testament Book of Daniel, and in the New Testament Book of Revelation he leads God's armies against Satan's forces where during the war in heaven he defeats Satan. It is in the Epistle of Jude, Michael is specifically referred to as 'the archangel Michael'. His name means 'who is like God?' and he is described as protector of Israel and leader of the armies of God.

The sculpture and its meaning is an incredibly powerful symbol that the work has been done by God in Jesus, and will be complete when things are made new, as the Revelation promises.

In all of this, we are to remember and be absolutely confident in this:

*For I am convinced that neither death, nor life, nor angels, nor rulers, nor things present, nor things to come, nor powers, nor height, nor depth, nor anything else in all creation, will be able to separate us from the love of God in Christ Jesus our Lord.*[39]

Amen.

# Mind The Gap
## Falling off the pedestal

If you've travelled on the London Underground system, then you have very likely heard the pre-recorded message at some stations as you attempt to leave the train – 'Mind the gap'. It is an audible and also visual warning to take caution of the gap between the train door and the station platform. If you fall, you will hurt yourself.

When you are a leader, the expectations are very high about you. You are to be perfect in every way. So ... heed the warning. Don't fall down the gap, or you will be damaged.

Leaders are very often put on pedestals. This is especially true if you are known as a leader who has a faith, and particularly if you have a Christian faith. If you are a leader who is doing 'a good job', then people will often describe you as 'wonderful'. You are so wonderful that all they see, with their blinkered eyes, is your good parts. These are the parts of you that are very public, and combined with their expectations, you are on a pedestal being displayed as a perfect person. Oh, how wrong they are!

Sometimes this high expectation of leaders comes from our theological understanding. This is especially the case if you are a priest leading a church. The view and understanding of priesthood, particularly in the Anglo-Catholic and Catholic Church, is that the priest is the 'icon of Christ'. An icon is that which points to Christ. Acknowledging that, as members of the church, all Christians share in Christ's unique priesthood, there is, however, a greater understanding of those who are priests. This is particularly the case when the Eucharist/Holy Communion/Lord's Supper is celebrated. The ordained priest is the sacramental representation of Christ the head and shepherd. In other words, the priest is a physical person, set apart and blessed to be the visual representation of Jesus Christ. Because Jesus was sinless, perhaps we might begin to understand why it is that some people have a huge expectation that their priest will therefore be the same.

There is, I believe quite rightly, the reality that if you take a leadership role, in whatever sphere of life, you must lead by example and realise that others will look to you (look up to you) to ascertain what is expected; what is right and wrong. We have to hold this expectation alongside St Peter, writing to the church in Rome, reminding them 'For there is no distinction, since all have sinned and fall short of the glory of God …'[40] There is no exception or exemption. Just because you are a leader, just because you are a church leader, just because you are an icon of Christ, the Great High Priest, does not make you eligible to be sinless, to be perfect. We are no different to anyone else. We are going to fall in the gap, and we are going to fall off the pedestal. Make no mistake about it.

When we are not perfect, it is often because of sin. What is sin? Simply an act that goes against the will of God. That 'will' was clearly communicated by Jesus before he died. He says '*I give you a new commandment, that you love one another. Just as I have loved you, you also should love one another.*'[41] This commandment sits alongside the other primary commandment: Jesus replies to one of the scribes when he is asked which commandment is the first of all? He says '*… you shall love the Lord your God with all your heart, and with all your soul, and with all your mind, and with all your strength. The second is this, you shall love your neighbour as yourself.*'[42] These two commandments are the foundation of faith in God and the standard for human living.

I remember that right back to the time when I was a teenager and involved in children's work, that I used to explain sin by saying that in the word sin, the letter 'I' was in the middle: the simple truth that when we put ourselves first, without a thought for God or others, then often 'I' becomes the centre, the reason, for sin.

God knows full well that we are imperfect and that we sin. I've said before that I believe, and experience, that God desires our intention. He knows if we are striving to live out those two commandments in our daily life. He knows if we are giving the command to love our best shot. And he knows that this side of heaven we are going to fail. And he is faithful to us. Guaranteed.

Within a few days of my life being turned upside down in a spectacular way, my wife and I were in our sitting room with a senior member of church leadership. I remember speaking openly, frankly and very honestly about what I thought (at the time) had happened to me. He said, 'Martin, I can't understand why you are being so honest with me. I have plenty of skeletons in the cupboard, and that is firmly where they are going to stay.' It was only as time passed by that both Pauline and I realised how disabling what he said actually is. When we hide away, supress our sins, or when we choose to put them to the back of our minds, life becomes exhausting. Doing as much as we can to pretend our sin does not exist uses our physical, spiritual and emotional energy in a way that is disabling and not life giving. In fact, it can lead to immense stress.

Eugene Peterson, in his paraphrase of the Bible, uses Paul's words in his letter to the Romans to say it far better than I ever could:

*It happens so regularly that it's predictable. The moment I decide to do good, sin is there to trip me up. I truly delight in God's commands, but it's pretty obvious that not all of me joins in that delight. Parts of me covertly rebel, and just when I least expect it, they take charge.*

*I've tried everything and nothing helps. I'm at the end of my rope. Is there no one who can do anything for me? Isn't that the real question? The answer, thank God, is that Jesus Christ can and does. He acted to set things right in this life of contradictions where I want to serve God with all my heart and mind, but am pulled by the influence of sin to do something totally different.*

*With the arrival of Jesus, the Messiah, that fateful dilemma is resolved. Those who enter into Christ's being-here-for-us no longer have to live under a continuous, low-lying black cloud. A new power is in operation. The Spirit of life in Christ, like a strong wind, has magnificently cleared the air, freeing you from a fated lifetime of brutal tyranny at the hands of sin and death.*

*God went for the jugular when he sent his own Son. He didn't deal with the problem as something remote and unimportant. In his Son, Jesus, he personally took on the human condition, entered the disordered mess of struggling humanity in order to set it right once and for all. The law code, weakened as it always was by fractured human nature, could never have done that.*

*The law always ended up being used as a Band-Aid on sin instead of a deep healing of it. And now what the law code asked for but we couldn't deliver is accomplished as we, instead of redoubling our own efforts, simply embrace what the Spirit is doing in us.*

*Those who think they can do it on their own end up obsessed with measuring their own moral muscle but never get around to exercising it in real life. Those who trust God's action in them find that God's Spirit is in them—living and breathing God! Obsession with self in these matters is a dead end; attention to God leads us out into the open, into a spacious, free life. Focusing on the self is the opposite of focusing on God. Anyone completely absorbed in self ignores God, ends up thinking more about self than God. That person ignores who God is and what he is doing. And God isn't pleased at being ignored.*

*But if God himself has taken up residence in your life, you can hardly be thinking more of yourself than of him. Anyone, of course, who has not welcomed this invisible but clearly present God, the Spirit of Christ, won't know what we're talking about. But for you who welcome him, in whom he dwells—even though you still experience all the limitations of sin—you yourself experience life on God's terms. It stands to reason, doesn't it, that if the alive-and-present God who raised Jesus from the dead moves into your life, he'll do the same thing in you that he did in Jesus, bringing you alive to himself? When God lives and breathes in you (and he does, as surely as he did in Jesus), you are delivered from that dead life. With his Spirit living in you, your body will be as alive as Christ's!*

*So, don't you see that we don't owe this old do-it-yourself life one red cent. There's nothing in it for us, nothing at all. The best thing to do is give it a decent burial and get on with your new life. God's Spirit beckons. There are things to do and places to go!*[43]

The totally gobsmacking, awesome reality is that God knows that we struggle with sin. We often sin, but God has done something amazing about putting that right – once and for all, in the death and resurrection of Jesus Christ. The act is a once and for all time event so that we will be forgiven sinners – we ARE forgiven sinners. That's how much God loves you, me and all his people, without exception and totally unconditionally.

The reality is that all leaders sin, and God knows. He sees it and hears it take place. Sometimes our sin is in our thoughts, our mind. Nevertheless, it is still sin. Sometimes those thoughts follow through to shape our actions. Those thoughts become so strong that we find it difficult and then impossible to hide them, and so they become public as we act them out to individuals and the wider community and world. Whilst our sinful thoughts and private actions are hidden (but still visible to God), other people will still continue to believe we are perfect. It is when our sin becomes public that judgement begins. People start judging us by our sin, mostly completely ignoring the fact that their judgement is sin too! Judgement is the powerful tool which knocks us off our pedestal, because when you are on the pedestal, the only place to go is down. We may even say, 'I'm going to knock them down a peg or two.' In other words, they need to come down in our estimation of them, or estimation of themselves.

The definition of judgement, in this context, is about making a considered decision, or to come to a sensible conclusion. That means we need to have all the facts in front of us, and we seldom do. That's why judging people is so dangerous, so sinful – because we will not have all the facts available to us to make an informed and considered decision. I suspect you, and definitely myself, have written someone off on looking at them, or after talking to them the first time. We blacklist them from our lives almost straight away. They are not good enough for us to be associated with. We decide, without knowing all the facts beforehand, either because of their personality traits, their looks, or their behaviour, to place them firmly under the pedestal, let alone on one, ready to be knocked off. I remember preaching a sermon with the overarching message of unconditional love. Judgement is a huge barrier to us loving others unconditionally. I challenged people to think about how they would react to various people sitting in a church building whom they regularly avoided contact. We had a guy who drank alcohol heavily. He wasn't a tramp, but would regularly be outside, often in the churchyard, drinking each day and sometimes getting to the point where he would shout obscenities. He didn't smell that great either. I asked people if they would go and sit next to him. Would they sit next to the teenager who used challenging language or in their eyes 'messed about'? Would they sit next to the person who had hurt them in some way? Would they sit next to the person who they disagreed with in some way? Jesus reminds us in no uncertain terms: 'Let anyone among you who is without sin be the first to throw a stone ...'[44] and also 'Why do you see the speck that is in your brother's eye, but do not notice the log that is in your own eye?'[45] It is so easy to see the faults and sin, in other people's lives, rather than acknowledge our own, to ourselves and before God. Or even treat something as sin when it is actually not.

The culture in which we now live subconsciously encourages us to make judgements about people and situations by what is said or written about in the media. The problem is that those forums are not providing us with all the facts to make an informed decision. We hear or read what is said and instantly make a judgement. That is not just naïve but highly dangerous. I know this to my great cost as I spectacularly fell off my pedestal. The media appears to often sensationalise the situation – particularly regarding the lives and actions of those in senior leadership positions. The media (in whatever form it comes) delights in knocking people who have fallen off their pedestal. Supposedly it sells more newspapers. We have witnessed it in recent years: Church leaders; sports personalities; musicians; television and film personalities; members of government; the monarchy. I am absolutely not saying that the general public should not be informed of somebody or group not behaving in an appropriate way, but more about the media not providing a more balanced and informed report. However, saying that, it is impossible for us to be completely informed and aware of all the facts. The onus is on us, as individuals, to know full well that we are not in a position to make a judgement when we do not know the reality or understand it. The danger is when we do so, we hurt whose who we judge, and also hurt ourselves because we have fallen into the trap of misinformed judgement. The only one with full knowledge to make a judgement is God. That's his business, not ours.

Whilst living in this world, we have to live with the potential tension of what God says about sin and what the law of the land has to say, which means we have to live with attempting to affect a balance. In God's eyes, a 'sin is a sin' against him. However large or small we might categorise a particular sin, they are equal in God's eyes. There are sins which have a greater effect on a human being than another: for example, if someone murders someone, then it has a devasting effect, not just on the one who is murdered, but to those who are hurt and effected by the action. However, if someone is called an unpleasant name, then it may have a lesser effect.

Humankind therefore, through the law, grades sin/wrongdoing and consequently the punishment is graded based on the sin/wrongdoing and effect on others. Let's not forget that in all of this, temptation is not a sin. Jesus was tempted by Satan in the dessert, but did not sin. Being tempted to murder someone is not a sin. It is when there is a decision made to allow the thought to turn into an action that the sin is committed. The letter of James reminds us: 'One is tempted by one's own desire, being lured and enticed by it; then, when that desire has conceived, it gives birth to sin, and that sin, when it is fully grown, gives birth to death. Do not be deceived, my beloved.' [46]

It would be understandable to be depressed by the reality that we are never going to be perfect (at least in this earthly life), and that (in the catchphrase words of Private Frazer from the classic television programme *Dad's Army*), we are 'all doomed'. There is no hope. But that is not true. Not one bit. Why? Because there is love, grace and forgiveness. And there is hope. When a friend knew that I was writing this chapter, she sent me the words of Julian of Norwich. They are the words that I have sent to others and have had sent to me. They are the words 'all shall be well, and all manner of thing shall be well.' However, I realised that I have been doing something with those words that I find deeply annoying about people quoting snippets of the Bible. They shorten the quote to fit their own need or point. My friend sent me the whole quotation, which changes the meaning and the context in a huge way. It says:

But Jesus, who in this vision informed me of all that is needed by me, answered with these words and said: 'It was necessary that there should be sin; but all shall be well, and all shall be well, and all manner of thing shall be well.'

As I mentioned earlier in the chapter – for now, we have to live with the reality that there is sin. We live, if you like, in 'the gap'. It is the gap between Jesus act of dying and rising so that sin and the devil is conquered and the time when we are resurrected too to the heavenly place where 'all things shall be made new'[47]. In other words, all is not 'doomed' because *'all shall be well, and all shall be well, and all manner of thing shall be well.'*

What about pedestals? I believe we have to concentrate on the foundation of our faith. We are commanded to love God and love one another – unconditionally. We are not called to like or agree with, or accept what someone may do which is wrong (a sin), but we must love them without making a judgement, and to love them unconditionally. There is no 'opt out clause' and no small writing at the bottom of the page that gives us terms and conditions. Love unconditionally.

What about trying to be perfect? With wisdom I have come to realise that God does not want us to be constantly stressed out trying to be perfect. In my dark days a friend sent me their daily reflection by Jon Bloom[48], who writes:

> *In Christ, you are free! You are free to follow Jesus imperfectly. You are free to fight the fight of faith defectively, because that's the only way you will ever fight for faith in this age.*

> *Perfectionism is a ponderous weight we must lay aside in the race of faith. God doesn't want us to focus on performing perfectly; he wants us to focus on living out a childlike, dependent faith through authentic acts of love.*

I say amen to that!

# The Mind Boggles
## Love, grace, mercy and forgiveness

The amazing reality is that God loves us unconditionally, gives us unlimited grace and forgives us constantly. Despite who we are and what we may have, or have not done. That's enough to make the mind boggle! By that, I mean that it doesn't make sense in human terms for that to be true. It seems at times impossible to comprehend or it could be described as just plain crazy. But it's true – and I know it.

At the age of six, whilst I was attending the local Church of England primary school, I was selected to sing in the choir at the church opposite. We lived in the grounds of the bishop's house as my father was the gardener. These three places no doubt put me in an inescapable faith environment. I can clearly remember singing in school assembly and church services this hymn – here are just the first two verses:

> God is love: His the care,
> Tending each, everywhere.
> God is love, all is there!
> Jesus came to show him,
> That mankind might know Him!
>
> None can see God above;
> We can share life and love;
> Thus may we Godward move,
> Seek him in creation,
> Holding every nation.[49]

Whilst in my old age I find the tune very annoying; the words are declaring a simple truth that I grew up with, and had no reason not to believe. I've wracked my brain to see if there were times when I didn't believe that truth, but I can't. Perhaps because nothing really dramatic happened in my life to make me question and doubt it. On reflection, overall, I was loved by many people and I was loving too. I fell in love with Pauline, my wife now, when I was about twenty years old. Love just 'was'.

It wasn't until I took part in the Ignatian Spiritual Exercises (explained and written about more in other chapters) that the truth that God is love started to develop. One Sunday morning during a church service I remember hearing the words that 'God loves me'. Not new, but the reality was explosive. I can only explain it by saying that this truth moved from my head to my heart and my whole being, in what seemed to be one complete swoop. It seemed and felt weird! I remember searching out my priest at the end of the service and sitting next to him trying to explain, I burst into tears. They were tears of a new experience. Tears from the very core of my being as though I was being cleansed, which seemed to go on for a long time. It was the most important and key part of my relationship with God. Yes, God is love, but now I absolutely knew that God loved me, loves me, so much so that he was in me and making that fact a reality. From head to heart and whole being.

Following that experience I was given a book which focused on a parable that I had heard hundreds of times. Written by Henri Nouwen, he speaks about his encounter with Rembrandt's painting of The Return of the Prodigal Son and how it started for him a long spiritual adventure. I read it and connected with it instantly. My experience above was echoed by Henri as I read:

> I cannot make myself feel loved. By myself I cannot leave the land of my anger. I cannot bring myself home nor can I create communion on my own. I can desire it, hope for it, wait for it, yes, pray for it. But my true freedom I cannot fabricate for myself. That must be given to me. I am lost. I must be found and brought home by the shepherd who goes out to me.[50]

This was all gift. I knew that I was loved by God. I received forgiveness without consciously asking, by grace and God's mercy. Wow! That was ultimate, unconditional, mind blowing and boggling, it was gobsmacking God in action. I will never forget it.

For me, that parable that Jesus speaks of, recorded by Luke[51], is the message of God in a nutshell. I am tempted to copy here the entire story, but please take time to read it with fresh and open eyes and heart in whatever Bible translation you prefer.

The story and the desire of homecoming needs to be heard and encountered by every one of us. For me, the most poignant part is the return encounter of the younger son with the father. Without words, as the compassionate father looks out and watches for his son's return, they embrace. They hug and there is a kiss. In this place, love and forgiveness, without being audibly asked for, are demonstrated in such a tangible way. Such is the character of God. Henri Nouwen writes of this place in such a personal way:

> It is a place of light, the place of truth, the place of love. It is the place where I so much want to be, but am so fearful of being. It is the place where I will receive all I desire, all that I ever hoped for, all that I will ever need, but it is also the place where I have to let go of all I most want to hold on to. It is the place that confronts me with the fact that truly accepting love, forgiveness, and healing is often much harder than giving it. It is the place beyond earning, deserving, and rewarding. It is the place of surrender and complete trust.[52]

For many, knowing that you are loved becomes a two-way action. Knowing God's love at this depth found me writing a poem (probably in its loosest sense!). I had never written one before and I have never written one since! In fact, I have never shared it until now. My journal on 20 December 1994 has pasted into it this:

> Creator God, I love you.
> For you flung the stars into the sky
> And made every living creature.
> Plans of beauty and splendour,
> All for the enjoyment of humankind.
> And you created me.
> You made me in your own image,
> Touched me, and brought me to life.
> You created me for yourself,
> That I may praise you and give you back my love.
> For you are great and marvellous,
> Mighty and awesome,
> And I love you.

*Jesus, my friend, I love you.*
*For you came as a baby in meekness*
*And yet you are the Son of God.*
*You lived a perfect human life,*
*And met a painful death on a cross.*
*All for me, because you love me.*
*You wiped away all my sin and conquered the devil.*
*All for me, because you love me.*
*And I am one with you, for I have died and risen again.*
*And I just want to praise you.*
*I want to walk with you and be close to you*
*And be more like you,*
*Because I love you.*

*Abba, Daddy, I love you.*
*For you welcome me with outstretched arms*
*You kiss me and give me your peace and your love.*
*You pick me up, holding me in your hand*
*That I may see you face to face.*
*You hold me close to your heart*
*That I may feel you and hear you.*
*You turn my weakness into your gentle strength*
*And I am out of control.*
*Out of control with my life and my love.*
*I surrender all that I am and all that I will be*
*Into your loving arms.*
*For I love you beyond telling.*[53]

Love demands a response. Whilst often it is a natural response to love God, and others in return for their love to me, to us, we cannot forget that it is also a command. Before Jesus meets his death, he gives two new commandments to his disciples. They are the overarching commandments of those given to Moses by God on Mount Sinai[54]. Jesus says:

*You shall love the Lord your God with all your heart, and with all your soul, and with all your mind... and... You shall love your neighbour as yourself.*[55]

Loving God and loving each other is energised, made possible by the Spirit of God who loves us. The disciple John, in his first letter writes

*We, though, are going to love—love and be loved. First, we were loved, now we love. He (God) loved us first. If anyone boasts, 'I love God,' and goes right on hating his brother or sister, thinking nothing of it, he is a liar. If he won't love the person he can see, how can he love the God he can't see? The command we have from Christ is blunt: Loving God includes loving people. You've got to love both.*[56]

Whilst all of this is true, it can also be extremely difficult to live out in practice. If we have experienced a difficult childhood or other relationships during which we felt unloved, or perhaps worse, then our understanding of love is tainted. God is big enough to work through that, often with the help of others such as counsellors and other professionals.

The reality of loving each other is challenging and hard work. Whilst working for an international horticultural company I often travelled to other countries. I remember a trip to our sister company in the USA and had to be there for a specific one-off meeting. There were problems in getting a seat with the airline I used to travel with but ended with a seat with Air India. The flight to New York was difficult with an eight-hour delay in departure, but the return trip seemed a whole lot worse. It was a whistle-stop trip, just forty-eight hours. I was tired already and as I stood in the queue for the check-in desk it was announced that there was a three-hour delay in departure. The airport was very hot and there were hundreds of others in the queue with me. I flipped in my mind, swearing at God for the stress and having others around me, and what seemed unbearable was the smell. I was not a happy person. As I stood, muttering, I was reminded of the time I had spent with a guy the previous Sunday. He had got into trouble and his court case was this week. He deeply regretted what he had done. He was in tears. He was hurting deeply as others called him names, some said they hated him and he felt unloved, not valued. I reminded him that I loved him and God loved him too. But here I was in an airport not loving those around me and blaming them for my situation. I said sorry to God and instantly he replied '*I love you beyond your sin*'. I still have a postcard which my priest gave me with those words on after I shared with him what happened. This is what God's love is. It is unconditional, full of grace, mercy and forgiveness. You and I have done, and will do, nothing to make it happen. It is all about God and all about what he does though his son Jesus, by his Holy Spirit. It is all grace. Philip Yancey reminds us in his book on the subject:

> There is nothing we can do to make God love us more.
>
> There is nothing we can do to make God love us less.[57]

Those two lines seem to explain what grace is about. God is graceful when we sin and when we feel we have failed.

Archbishop Justin Welby shares this story to illustrate further:

> A Swiss friend of mine, who gave up a life in politics and the law to become a hermit and now leads a remarkable religious community, often says 'c'est tout grace' (it's all grace): what we receive is a gift that we have not earned and for which we must account. We are stewards. At the heart of Christian discipleship is to know is that all we have is gift, and to live out that knowledge. To understand that 'all is grace' is to know that what we receive is the providence of God: God's love freely given in tangible forms.[58]

We are to display and act with grace. Grace is founded on love, and grace is bound up with mercy. We are to be merciful just as God is merciful to us,[59] and is worked out in our lives through acts of kindness, empathy and compassion, not being offended and selflessly bringing a bit of light into a dark situation.

Love, grace and mercy lead to forgiveness. Thomas Merton wrote:

> God has left sin in the world in order that there may be forgiveness: not only the secret forgiveness by which He Himself cleanses our souls, but the

*manifest forgiveness by which we have mercy on one another and so give expression to the fact that He is living, by his mercy, in our own hearts.*[60]

Forgiveness is on a level with love, grace and mercy. Not one of these are optional extras if we profess to have a Christian faith. Each of them is unconditionally actioned by God to everyone, and we are to do the same. Lots of us say the words of the Lord's Prayer which includes the line that we forgive others as we are asking God to forgive our wrongdoing (a.k.a. sin). God forgiving us and our forgiving each other is bound together. There is to be no limit to the times we forgive, even if it is tiresome or makes us angry — in the same way that God goes on forgiving us without counting or reminding us.

It will be no surprise that I am saying that forgiving others is not easy. I believe what I have written in the previous paragraph wholeheartedly. There have been serious times over the last few years when people have hurt me badly, through their actions and what they have said, to my face, but mostly behind my back. I am sure there are times when I have unknowingly hurt others by being too busy, or tired, or focussed on what I saw was another priority. I'm sure it will be true for you too. This is often the case, especially if you are in a leadership role. People expect you to be nice to them, but can find it unforgiving if you treat them in ways they don't expect. We know all too well that we all have the ability to say, think and do things which are wrong. That which is not pleasing to God, or to another human being. But the fact, the command, remains the same. We are to forgive one another.

The fundamental core here is that we are commanded to love each other for who we are. We are not commanded to love what each other may do. That is true of God also. Once again, the building block for forgiveness is love. If we struggle to love ourselves, sometimes because we do not know what it is to be loved, then we may also not really know what it is to be forgiven by God and the people around us. Making judgements about people also comes into play — a subject I have written about elsewhere. That too is a sinful act on our behalf. How do we know what is going on in the life of the person who has hurt us? How do we know the circumstances of how they reacted?

Whilst my own wrongdoing was very public, I chose to write with a contrite heart, a very open/public letter of explanation as to the circumstances. I apologised and said how very sorry I was for the hurt that people had experienced because of my actions. I naïvely thought that people would begin to forgive me. Many did, for which I thank them. A few were fuelled by others to manipulate the facts I had written about, insinuating that they were lies. They were absolutely not. Four couples, who were very good and close friends, chose to turn their backs on Pauline and I. Some, I know, destroyed the letter or filed it, opting out of any response from them. I wonder if they have said the Lord's Prayer since? I'm also aware that some priests have said that you have to be ready to forgive. That can be a cop-out and leave people to try and get out of the act. Take time, yes, but not too long.

I understood in the early days, and now, that people were hurt by my actions and felt very let down, for which I am truly sorry. My family had to deal with the immense hurt of people walking away or telling blatant lies about me and the situation, sometimes by leaders of the institutional church. They encountered a lack of support and love, when they were innocent of any wrongdoing. Individual and group counselling helped me greatly, particularly when I was in a dark place which enveloped my whole being. The love and support of those who were, and are, friends and family were crucial, and still is now. They have exhibited the love, grace, mercy and forgiveness of God, sometimes at great personal cost. Thank you so much.

Counselling taught me how to put myself in other people's shoes, particularly the individuals in the four couples. What was going on in their lives? What did my actions trigger in their life? What pressure was put on them by others that they gave way to? Did they find themselves protecting themselves first and foremost? I will probably never know. But I have forgiven them for not forgiving me, or supporting me when I needed it the most. The scar of the hurt is still there, and will always be. Getting to that point of forgiveness is very healing. It is a place of freedom, a place of letting go. If you have not got to that point and think that you have buried it all in the deep recesses of your mind ... beware, for it will debilitate your freedom and often that which is buried erupts into a volcano of mental and spiritual illness that can also result in physical illness. Please be brave to deal with it and seek help from those you trust that are wise and professional.

When I am able, I buy a copy of *The Big Issue*. I love having a chat with the person I buy it from and I know that she will get a percentage of the money she takes to live on. In the Christmas issue 2019 there was an interview with Archbishop Justin Welby. The last question he was asked was 'What is your Christmas message to the country?' He replied

*Don't fear. Deal with fear. In the New Testament, among the letters from John, it says 'perfect love casts our fear'. So love, don't fear. Because the kind of love that God shows is a love that doesn't expect return. That forgives failure. That loves people despite their ups and downs. That kind of love changes the world in a dramatic and wonderful way. And it is wonderful and not patronising or paternalistic towards those who have fallen off the edge for whatever reason – whether it's because of something they have done or something that was done to them. God doesn't make that distinction. He just says: 'If you've fallen off the edge, I am with you. I come to you; I love you.' And the way he does that is through our heads and hearts and our eyes and our generosity in caring for people. So don't fear, love.*[61]

We have to remember and be faithful to the fact that God's love, grace, mercy and forgiveness are acted out through us. How are others to know this is what God does, if we do not do it ourselves? Archbishop Welby has that fantastic message of truth. I am so sad, that for me and my family, the institution that the Archbishop leads was not true to what I know he believes and desires. The preservation of institution and self came before being Christlike. Thank goodness, thank God, some people are willing. Some with faith, some who say they have none. Risky!

*Wherever love is, there is God.*
*What kind of love is God's love?*
*It is a love which forgives..*
*And then forgives..*
*And forgives again.*
*It is a love which rolls up its sleeves*
*And gets involved in caring*
*And mending and building.*
*It is a love which is quite happy*
*To be considered a fool*
*To be considered weak.*
*It is a love which goes on giving*
*But keeps no accounts.*
*Love that is non-selective*
*And uncompromising.*
*This is the nature of God's love*
*For this is the nature of our God*
*Revealed in Jesus Christ our Lord.*[62]

# Mind Blowing
## Full of potential

Let's start by going backwards! Once upon a time ... or should I say ... In the beginning ...

Eugene Peterson's paraphrase of the Bible[63] puts it like this:

*First this: God created the Heavens and Earth – all you see, all you don't see. Earth was a soup of nothingness, a bottomless emptiness, an inky blackness. God's Spirit brooded like a bird above the watery abyss.*

*God spoke: 'Light' and light appeared. God saw that light was good and separated light from dark...'[64]*

And so, the story of creation begins. You may take the account in Genesis literally, or see it in another way. Whatever – the overall belief is about God as creator, creating the world in which we live. God goes on from creating light to create so much more. He is clearly delighted with what he achieves, as repeatedly we are told, 'God saw that it was good'. He was having the time of his life and revelling in it! We are then told:

*Heaven and Earth were finished, down to the last detail.[65]*

And after God has a rest, this is what he does next:

*At the time God made earth and Heaven, before any grasses or shrubs had sprouted from the ground—God hadn't yet sent rain on earth, nor was there anyone around to work the ground (the whole earth was watered by underground springs)—God formed Man out of dirt from the ground and blew into his nostrils the breath of life. The Man came alive—a living soul!...*

*GOD took the Man and set him down in the Garden of Eden to work the ground and keep it in order.*[66]

Enter Adam on the scene. But God doesn't stop there.

*GOD said, 'It's not good for the Man to be alone; I'll make him a helper, a companion.' So GOD formed from the dirt of the ground all the animals of the field and all the birds of the air. He brought them to the Man to see what he would name them. Whatever the Man called each living creature, that was its name. The Man named the cattle, named the birds of the air, named the wild animals; but he didn't find a suitable companion.*

*GOD put the Man into a deep sleep. As he slept he removed one of his ribs and replaced it with flesh. GOD then used the rib that he had taken from the Man to make Woman and presented her to the Man.*[67]

God creating man and woman, but I wonder how many times we have really read those sentences and reflected on them. This is amazing stuff.

I like listening to and reading what Rob Bell has to say. He was the founding pastor of Mars Hill Bible Church in Grandville, Michigan and considers faith 'outside the box', looking at it afresh and not afraid to share his thoughts. I can completely identify with that approach. Anyway, Rob is also a writer and presenter. Some of his teaching uses short films. In a series called NOOMA[68], my favourite film from the series is called *Breathe*. It is in talking about who we are – that he says this

*... we've been breathed into by the creator of the universe, and this divine breath is in every single human being ever. Like it's written in the Psalms ... Psalms 8 says that, 'God has crowned us with glory and honour.' Glory and honour in this passage isn't referring to God, it's referring to the people God has made. We're these sacred, divine, dirt clods, and yet we possess untold power and strength.*

Seriously – just stop and reflect on how he articulates what we hear in the Book of Genesis. I find it mind blowing, and that which blows our minds intensely affects our mind and our emotions. That which is mind blowing has to affect us as it connects to the mind of Christ.

God creates us with these two seemingly contrasting aspects. We are created from the dust of the ground but we are also given the breath of God. The vulnerability and fragility and the power of God in harmony.

The Church of England sometimes uses these words as part of the main prayer at communion:

> *From the beginning you have created all things and all your works echo the silent music of your praise. In the fullness of time you made us in your image, the crown of all creation.*[69]

God does not see his creation of us as 'good' but we are the crown, the pinnacle of God's work of creation. He delights in us. Why? Simply because we have his breath in us. There is no closer relationship possible. Saint Paul, preaching in the meeting of the Areopagus[70] tells them:

> *The God who made the world and everything in it, he who is Lord of heaven and earth, does not live in shrines made by human hands, nor is he served by human hands, as though he needed anything, since he himself gives to all mortals life and breath and all things. From one ancestor he made all nations to inhabit the whole earth, and he allotted the times of their existence and the boundaries of the places where they would live, so that they would search for God and perhaps grope for him and find him—though indeed he is not far from each one of us. For 'In him we live and move and have our being'[71]; as even some of your own poets have said, 'For we too are his offspring.'*[72]

The poet, quoted by Paul, sums up for us who we are and what our identity is. We are in God, as God is in us. Inseparable. It is as we go about our lives that we have our being. As we go about our life journey we continue to form our very being – who we are. Whilst I firmly believe from experience that God is in everyone, each of our life journeys will be different. It is this which makes each one of us totally and utterly unique. There was, and never will be, another one of us!

For over fifty years I was fortunate enough to have a fairly easy and normal life until the devastating time when, during illness, I found myself committing a crime. (I write elsewhere more about that time.) Because of my leadership role the media were very keen to report on it (understandably so), but what is available to read about me is very far-short of the entire truth. I am in a very different place now – mentally strong and fully recovered and with great understanding of how I managed to find myself in that dark place. Being then the centre of media attention, the main thing I wanted to do was to hide. I even spent quite a few months with a beard – I think trying to disguise myself from others, but also trying to hide and deny myself of the person I had become. A few years later it was suggested to me that I might like to change my name, something which people often do, particularly when wanting to start a new chapter of their life. I spent a great deal of time thinking and reflecting on various options. Doing either of them, for me, would deny what happened but more importantly would deny my true identity. I chose to do neither. It was a very small period of time in my life, and is something that I would never have wished to encounter – but I have. The experience of the time leading up to it, and that which followed, has been life changing, transformative, and a great deal of 'good' has come from it. It has been, and is, part of who I am, warts and all. All of our life is lived in God and who we are being continually shaped by what we do in our life. Because God is more than okay with that, so am I. Out of weakness God has brought strength. From darkness there is the light of opportunities.

Jesus' life on earth was far from easy and that should give us confidence to know that God is aware of how me might feel when we find ourselves in such situations. That 'God knowledge' is very close to us. Joyce Meyer reminds us

> Jesus displayed a positive outlook and attitude. He endured many difficulties and personal attacks – being lied about, being deserted by His disciples when He needed them most, being made fun of, being lonely, misunderstood, and a host of other discouraging things. Yet in the midst of all these negatives He remained positive. He always had an uplifting comment, an encouraging word; He always gave hope to all those He came near. [73]

It can be very easy to say to someone struggling that they are to remain positive. I've had people say that to me and rightly so. We have to remember that God is a god of that which is possible not impossible. God's transformative power is immense. Surrounding ourselves in difficult times with people who know the God of possibilities, faithfulness, love, forgiveness and so much more, is key. Because of who we are in God, the potential for us is off the scale (in a good way)! I have used this poem myself, and for others, often:

*Our deepest fear is not that we are inadequate.*
*Our deepest fear is that we are powerful beyond measure.*
*It is our light, not our darkness*
*That most frightens us.*
*We ask ourselves*
*Who am I to be brilliant, gorgeous, talented, fabulous?*
*Actually, who are you not to be?*
*You are a child of God.*
*Your playing small*
*Does not serve the world.*
*There's nothing enlightened about shrinking*
*So that other people won't feel insecure around you.*
*We are all meant to shine,*
*As children do.*
*We were born to make manifest*
*The glory of God that is within us.*
*It's not just in some of us;*
*It's in everyone.*
*And as we let our own light shine,*
*We unconsciously give other people permission to do the same.*
*As we're liberated from our own fear,*
*Our presence automatically liberates others.*[74]

Never allow apathy or procrastination, or fear of failure to stop you pursuing what you believe is right. Jump in with both feet! If you are in a leadership role, that is so important. We can dream about what is right, we can talk about it, and make the excuse that we have to pray about it for a long time – but God raises up leaders to get on and do it. Because of who we are in God we can be absolutely confident, and even if we get it wrong, by being close to God, helps to discern that which is right. Think big. Think God.

# Cast Your Mind Back
## Reflection and prayer

The concept of reflection is, to most people, a natural part of everyday life. It is part of our human makeup in which our mind recalls conversations, events and thoughts. We either allow that process to continue and develop, or we consciously decide that we don't want to think about something at the moment, and put it back in the part of our brain that retains information.

I would dare to suggest that all prayer begins with active reflection. By prayer, I simply mean a conscious interaction with God. I'll 'flesh that out' more during the chapter. I am not ignoring what is often called intercessory prayer – praying for ourselves and for, and on behalf of, others. This style of prayer is often described as 'shopping list' prayers, where we have a list of people and things, and work our way through them asking God to do something about them. These are either privately prayed or shared aloud in public places, such as during acts of worship. So, please just bear with me.

Over the years I have read countless books on prayer, led seminar and training days, retreat days, and been a spiritual director/friend/mentor to many. There seems to be a misdirection about Christian prayer. We seem to think that we have to be dutiful in the act, and the more we are, the more points from God we amass. We think we are like an Olympic athlete. We must exercise every day to achieve the required goal. It is our responsibility and our necessary chore for union with God, we think. Sadly, I have heard far too often church leaders be dictatorial about the required prayer and Bible reading that must be done every day. Thinking that God will be displeased if we don't do that, or that he won't communicate to us any other way, could not be further from the truth. There is a real danger in treating prayer as a discipline for spiritual excellence. The Christian life is not the Olympics and God is not looking for elite performers. In prayer we encounter the liberating truth that God has low standards – honestly! God has no interest in our plans for spiritual perfection. Rather than a duty, prayer should be approached as one of the most natural and often pleasurable experiences in our life. Trying to pretend that we are praying correctly by saying the right words in the right order is only kidding ourselves, and God is well-aware of how we really feel. Praying with rules is false and can add to our stress level.

Be liberated and chill out! Prayer is ultimately about the way we relate and communicate to God – and it is a two-way encounter. Our prayer needs to be the natural response of how we are, and where we are, in our relationship with God. That can manifest itself in a vast number of ways.

Let me return now to reflection. After all, I began by saying that our prayer arises from our reflection. It wouldn't be unreasonable to say that they are intrinsically together.

Reflection is about recalling what we have encountered: what has been done, said, seen, questioned, how we feel and reacted – in other words, what has been going on in our life. Reflection generates our intercessory prayer, mentioned earlier by recalling information that we have received, in whatever way.

One of the key aspects of Ignatian Spirituality[75] is that it acknowledges that God is constantly present and active in our world. It is the act of reflection that helps us to discover when we have encountered God and the context that it was in. We might even call them 'burning bush moments' – moments as Moses encountered when he met God in the flames of a burning bush. The poet R S Thomas[76], in the poem *The Bright Field*, puts it beautifully:

> *I have seen the sun break through*
> *to illuminate a small field*
> *for a while, and gone my way*
> *and forgotten it. But that was the pearl*
> *of great price, the one field that had*
> *treasure in it. I realise now*
> *that I must give all that I have*
> *to possess it. Life is not hurrying*
> *on to a receding future, nor hankering after*

*an imagined past. It is the turning*
*aside like Moses to the miracle*
*of the lit bush, to a brightness*
*that seemed as transitory as your youth*
*once, but is the eternity that awaits you.*

Reflection is a method to help us ask the question 'Where did I encounter the burning bush today?' and ask God to help us mindfully recall those times. There may be occasions when we are, thankful, disappointed, puzzled, invigorated, angry ... I'm sure you understand what I am saying? Acknowledging all our emotions is being honest before God. It is not a time for beating ourself up if we have not loved others, loved our self or loved God. Yes, you may need to claim God's forgiveness, but that happens instantly from God, so move on. What comes out of those times you may find helpful to write down; generate lists, write a journal, poetry, prayers and so on. More ideas of how you can do that are written about below. Finding the opportunities to do that are always rewarding. I went through a long period in my life where I would do that at the end of each day. However, the end of the day when we are exhausted is not a good choice, so perhaps the following morning. But the key thing here is to do it when is right for you, even if that is once a week, or longer. The way in which you choose to do it is also exclusively yours: perhaps during a walk, jogging, sitting in silence, laying down ... whilst driving the car can be risky!

Allowing prayer to rise from our reflection can come from other ways too, such as reading. The apostle Paul, writing to Timothy reminds us:

*All scripture is God-breathed and is useful for teaching, rebuking, correcting and training in righteousness ...*[77]

Reading the Bible attentively, reading slowly, and with the expectation that God has spoken through these words for thousands of years can be spiritually enlightening. It is not just reading the words for information but rather doing so as if God is saying the words to you. If a word or words connect with you, hold on to it, slowly repeating it to yourself and allowing it to interact with what is going on in your life at that time. Prayer may then arise from that, or you may repeat the exercise another day if that seems right for you. This is an ancient monastic method called *lectio divina* or holy reading. Reading books, poetry, prayers, meditations, letters, and more, can be done in exactly the same way.

Music is another fantastic gift to encourage our reflection. God is not selective about the genre of music you listen to – if he wants to speak through it, he will!

Allowing all our senses to stimulate our reflection provides a rich smorgasbord of activity. The sense of smell, such as in some church traditions using incense; the smell of bread and wine at Holy Communion; the smell of fresh air or the smell of cool rain on hot ground; the perfume of flowers and so much more; receiving a hug, or the touch of someone's hand on ours; holding a cross, a stone or an item which is personal to you.

What we see has a vastness. Enjoying creation through walking; sitting for a good period of time; spending time with people, not just those we know, but also with those who challenge us and make us feel uncomfortable; watching drama such as films or scenes from Jesus' life; opera and musicals. We can also take pictures and use them to reflect on again later, or share them with someone else.

When our reflection leads into prayer it does not just have to be in the form of words (prewritten or spontaneous), but can be expressed in drawing, colouring pictures, painting, collage and sculpture. I have had the enormous privilege over the years to be alongside people at key parts of their faith journey. Using interactive and visual ways to make such times are mind-blowingly spiritually powerful. I spent months and months listening and sharing the pain of a mother whose daughter had died at a very young age. The experience brought depression, isolation, difficult family relationships, anger with God, lack of self-worth and belief. She was stuck in a dark hole that felt permanent. After so many hours she arrived at a point where she wanted to move on but did not know how. I took her one afternoon to a quiet rural church where she spent time writing desires, questions, feelings, confessions and allowing her mind to empty out on to the individual pieces of paper. A candle was lit on the alter and we took the papers and one by one set fire to them (placing them in a tin tray). When it was complete, I immediately encouraged her to walk out of the building with me, taking the tin of burned papers with us. Outside we allowed the wind to blow the ashes away. It was a spiritually and emotional time, with tears shed of cleansing, forgiveness and more. A recognition that all she shared had now been consumed in the fire of God's love and a new chapter of her life began. She went on later to work with the bereaved.

The act of burning is finite. I journeyed with a young guy who carried the baggage of his past life which was holding him back from being affirmed for who he was. In his isolation he would draw and write in plain workbooks, and for years they were kept under his bed. I cannot even count the hours that led to the point where he was ready to let the past go. We sat together one day in our lounge, in front of the log fire, where he tore up each page of the books and allowed the fire to acknowledge that God had received his past and he was ready for the future.

These are just two of the precious times when people have allowed their reflection (sometimes over years and months) to turn their prayer into that which is powerfully visual. The youth project that we ran was mostly held in the church building. In the large chapel, in one part of the building, there was a large notebook with things to write with. Many young people believed that God was real but struggled with prayer said in their minds but often wrote the prayers down as a way to express themselves, knowing that when they left the building, God had received their prayer. Over a few years there were so many prayers. Here is just one of them:

*Dear God*

*Please help me change. I have been so horrible to people in the past and I just want the strength to change. I am sorry for/to everyone I have hurt or said something out of order to. I don't want to be like this. I do try but I have had so many things happen this year, e.g., my parents split up. My dad was finally cured of leukaemia and I just want to be strong & help them get through everything as a family and so many people have helped me through things this year, like RG, JB, KK, MM, MH, AB & all of my friends. And I just want people to realise I am trying to change and I am sorry for everything. Most of all I want people to trust me please. I'm sorry again ... but thanks to RG, O & A & all my friends I'm getting there.*

*Thanks, JC*

*And also, I would like you to help me to control my anger and not lose it, especially with my mum who does everything. … and also, I want my behaviour to change. At the moment I have stupid moments as well. My moments where I feel grown up and I would like everyone to realise I am changing from a boy to a man and that they can trust me. Also, to look out for me and my friends … and all the others as well as me. Thank you. Amen!*

Allowing prayer to arise from silence has been practised since ancient times, particularly the mystics.[78] For most people, it does not come naturally and takes some time to develop. Finding ourselves in a silent place, both physically and also in our own soul can be refreshing and affirming. I used to call these times 'wasting time with God'. They are really not wasteful, but it is a bit like laying on the sofa with the one you love and not needing to say anything to each other for the whole evening. Simply chilling out in the space and secure that the one you are with loves you and accepts you for who you are. The songwriter gathers together what I am trying to say:

> *Be still for the presence of the Lord*
> *The Holy One is here*
> *Come bow before Him now*
> *With reverence and fear*
> *In Him no sin is found*
> *We stand on holy ground*
> *Be still for the presence of the Lord*
> *The Holy One is here*
>
> *Be still for the glory of the Lord*
> *Is shining all around*
> *He burns with holy fire*
> *With splendour He is crowned*
> *How awesome is the sight*
> *Our radiant King of light*
> *Be still for the glory of the Lord*
> *Is shining all around*[79]

The practice of mindfulness is centred on silence too and I've said more on that elsewhere.

Carlo Carretto, an Italian mystic who went into the desert to pray, writes this in his book:

> So true prayer demands that we be more passive than active; it requires more silence than words, more adoration than study, more concentration than rushing about, more faith than reason. We must understand thoroughly that true prayer is a gift from heaven to earth, the Father to his child; from the Bridegroom to the bride, from he who has, to him who has not, from everything to nothing.[80]

I've said that silence can be really difficult for some people, for all sorts of reasons. Placing ourselves into silence is in our control, but when we reflect and pray and cannot seem to find God's response we understandably ask, 'Why had God gone silent on me?' When writing about discernment I mentioned a quote that described God's silence as his activity whilst 'moving the furniture' for the next chapter of our lives. Provided that we find the opportunities for our reflection, using all of our senses to discern what God is saying, then that is enough. We have to wait patiently for what comes next. This is, of course a much bigger subject than I have room for here! There is a fantastic book called *God on Mute* [81] by Pete Greig that covers so many aspects and makes helpful suggestions. It's a good read!

Reflection and prayer in our everyday life can be very diverse in the way we encounter it but there are times when a longer period of time can be beneficial. Taking time to retreat from everyday life, often with no hidden agenda, except to chill out in the company of God. It may be for a day, weekend or longer – whatever is right for you. There are several venues which specialise in offering hospitality and, should you want it, someone who will meet with you each day to share in your time and reflect with you. The Retreat Association[82] is a great place to see what is available. I have always known God to be faithful in making such times a blessing. He responds to the fact that we desire to meet him more deeply and we will sacrifice time to do so. Jesus frequently took time out to retreat and encouraged those around him to do the same. Mark recalls:

*The apostles gathered around Jesus, and told him all that they had done and taught. He said to them, 'Come away to a deserted place all by yourselves and rest a while.' For many were coming and going, and they had no leisure even to eat. And they went away in the boat to a deserted place by themselves.*[83]

Henri Nouwen, in his small book on leadership concurs:

*We have indeed to fashion our own desert where we can withdraw every day, shake off our compulsions, and dwell in the gentle healing presence of our Lord. Without such a desert, we will lose our own soul while preaching the Gospel to others.*[84]

The ways in which you can reflect and pray are not exhaustive here and many books have been written sharing ideas, experience and offering more detail.

When we reflect and our prayer rises out of that act, know with confidence that God is there to hear your prayer, as certain as your next breath. Our whole lives are prayer. Don't work yourself up to pray but allow it to be the most natural activity and realise that it is completely gifted to you from God.

# What's On Your Mind?
## Speaking and listening

It doesn't matter if you have a faith or not – the fact remains that we were not created to be alone. In the account of creation, God creates a man (Adam), and God tells Adam that it is not good for man to be alone, and so he creates a helper, a companion, Eve.[85] The man and the woman go on to have children and humankind begins. God is the instigator of relationships. He creates humankind to be in relationship with him and that includes humankind being in relationship with each other. God needs us and we need God, and we need each other. I believe that it is the combination of all these relationships that enables us to claim the gift of life and live it to the full.

The British are well known for 'bottling things up'! Historically we gained that way of living from teachings at school. It was good to show strength of character and resolve in adversity. Then there is the well-known motivational poster by the British Government in 1939, in preparation for World War II – *Keep Calm and Carry On*. It's not 'the done thing' to show weakness, tears, share our emotions and telling someone how we feel – it might show that we are feeble. We need to get a grip. Much better to bottle things up. Thank goodness that way of living is declining, but it does not seem to come naturally to us to share what is going on in our life with others. That maybe about admitting weakness or perhaps making ourselves vulnerable and not trusting others who might hurt us. The other thing that we are afraid of is thinking that if we talk about things which have been buried in our mind for some time, that 'opening the lid of the box of our mind means we will probably never put the lid back on'.

The old British Telecom adverts declared 'It's good to talk', and in 1995 the key message included reminding us about 'having the time to listen' because it 'makes the world go round'. Speaking and listening are two of our senses that are key to the gift of communication. I cannot recommend highly enough the act of talking with someone, and particularly someone who is detached from the context that you are in. I am not recommending it because I'm brilliant at doing it, but the act and the intention is a good and healthy one. The old saying of 'a problem shared is a problem halved' is helpful. Sharing your life journey with someone else is very often a healing experience. You can talk to yourself and go over and over in your mind what you are concerned about, but when you actually hear yourself form the words to talk to another person, your mind becomes freer, stress begins to be relieved and a new part of your journey begins.

Who might we talk to? There are a number of descriptions for people, such as mentor, soul mate/friend, spiritual director, spiritual friend. The key attribute of who you choose is trust. Can I trust the person that I am talking to? Will they keep confidentiality? Some businesses have a mentor scheme, but, as I said earlier, it may be better to find someone out of your immediate context to preserve trust. That is simply because some businesses will still report back some aspect of your conversations.

In the time of exploring my call to be a priest[86], and all through my time as a priest and church leader, I had a spiritual director. Being in the Church of England, I chose a Roman Catholic woman who lived about twenty miles away. Her role was to listen attentively to what was going on in my life since the last time we met – a kind of unpacking of what was on my mind. She would reflect back to me what she was hearing and asked questions, sometimes for clarification or additional information. She would offer some suggestions; challenge me; encourage me; pray for me. She would listen to me ranting about the people and situations that annoyed and frustrated me; share in my joys and excitement; and work with me as I was discerning what God was saying and leading me to. I trusted her implicitly and am deeply grateful for her time, freely given, her wisdom and knowledge and complete confidentiality. It must have been worthwhile as I continued to do that almost once a month for over twenty years.

Choosing a person is very often not easy. In institutional church settings the first port of call might be asking colleagues if they have any experience in this area, or know of someone else to approach. There are occasionally people who specialise in spirituality within the organisational structure. The Spiritual Direction Network[87] has a useful website to look at.

Whoever you choose, it should always be agreed that at any point, any of the two people can end the relationship. It is a matter of discerning on both sides if this is right at that point in time and should never be taken personally if the arrangement comes to an end.

Forming for yourself a support network team is a great thing to do too. A mentor/spiritual director may be one of that team around you. I have already suggested in the chapters on discernment, and also on vision, that selecting a few people to consult is incredibly helpful. Mentors are also good to have, especially if you are new to a particular role or organisation. If there are particular issues identified, then professionals, such as a counsellor, may be appropriate for a period of time. When I was going through my mental breakdown, I was assigned a pastoral bishop. For me, it was a retired bishop – one who was extremely wise and certainly God given, as he understood my spirituality. I certainly needed someone who was a priest, had great experience of the role of a priest, and one who would not be judgemental, as the institution had been. I particularly wanted to have someone to reflect with who would do so theologically. I use that word in the understanding of 'helping me to see God in the world, God in my situations (past, present and to come) and God in my life and whole being'. I am, again, hugely grateful for him journeying with me over that period of time.

Talking to those that you love and are close to you is, of course, essential. However, it may be that there are things which cannot be said, such as details of situations in employment, or aspects of relationships that are just not the right time to share with that particular person. Living through my own time of extreme stress I found myself doing things which were not in my character or right mind. As this developed, I knew that I needed to talk to someone about it, but as I became immersed in what I knew afterwards was a mental breakdown, I didn't trust anyone to talk to. I thought that if I talked with my wife, then she would no longer love me and I certainly didn't trust the institution that I was part of. Through counselling later, I realise that this perpetuated a deep-seated lack of self-worth. I knew it was right to talk to someone but in the dark place that I found myself, I could not see a way out. This is why I mentioned earlier that talking with others is so important, but I am not always good at it. At least, I wasn't during that part of my life.

Whilst speaking with others is essential, so is listening. I am using the word listening, rather than hearing. I suspect that most of us have said to someone, 'You might be hearing me, but you're not listening to me.' There is a difference in what these two words mean. Hearing is about receiving and perceiving sounds. Listening is about paying attention to the sounds and in this case, connecting to the person who is talking to you, hearing with thoughtful attention and considering what is being said.

When we really listen to someone, we give them value, acknowledging their worth. If we are listening to someone speak about what is going on in this life, past or present, or even desires for the future, we become available to them, and we offer this incredible gift within the busyness of noise and of daily life. This gift of listening also needs to combine our sense of watching (if we are able): watching facial expression, making eye contact, watching hands and gestures. What we listen to, and see, helps us discern what is right to speak.

Within the act of speaking and listening we should not be afraid of silence. It is so important to allow someone to finish what they are saying before we reply. If we are not sure what to say, it is far better to allow silence than to find wrong words, or words of platitude and small-talk. Sometimes the more we say, the less we hear.

When I have spoken about experiences and feelings, I have sometimes experienced my 'pet hate' – hearing the other person say, 'I know just how you feel.' Aaaargh – 'No you don't!' You may have experienced something similar in your own context, but not in exactly the same way as someone else. Plus, there are people who want to reply by starting to talk about their life and hijacking the conversation to turn the focus on them. However, sometimes it is right to take an example from our own lives, but it should never take long to share. Whilst I'm on the 'don't do' list: don't interrupt someone, offer critical explanations, judge them, or make swift conclusions. A great many times people have said to me 'Thank you for listening. I just needed to know that someone else knows what is going on for me at the moment.' Often, we don't need to say anything as a response. The act of listening is what is needed.

Listening to difficult things going on in people's lives can be burdensome, particularly if you are doing that as a professional. I spent twenty years as a parish priest listening to people share confessions and very deep and personal things. For me, that continues still as my calling to be a priest in a very different way. Coming away from listening to someone has often led me to desperately want to fix their life for them, to put a 'sticky plaster' on for them, pat their head, and tell them that 'everything is okay now'. Even as a priest we are not Jesus Christ, here to save other people. Yes, Jesus Christ may work through us as we work in partnership, but it must never be a burden to take on others' challenges in life. Hence, professionals must always have someone to talk to themselves, but never should people's names be used, which is why having someone out of your own area of living and context is wise. Again, I'm saying what is a right and good thing to do, but there were times when I should have done that and didn't. It is so easy to keep going and listening to people because they need you to be there for them, but effective listening means taking ways to ensure that the burden is light.

Listening to others is made easier when we are able to listen to ourselves and listen to God. I have written quite a bit in the chapter on reflection and prayer so won't repeat myself. However, I only mentioned elsewhere the practice of mindfulness, so here is a little more about it. Listening to ourselves means that we need to be present – present to what is going on at a particular point or period of time. As human beings it is not a natural activity and so we need to train ourselves to focus, to calm ourselves. I am aware that many people practise mindfulness who do not have a faith, but for me, the practice becomes richer with the knowledge that God is present too. There is a richly written little book entitled *The Sacrament of the Present Moment*[88] which helps in explaining the reality that God is present at every moment of every day. Jean-Pierre De Caussade writes profoundly

*The present moment holds infinite riches beyond your wildest dreams but you will only enjoy them to the extent of your faith and love. The more a soul loves, the more it longs, the more it hopes, the more it finds. The will of God is manifest in each moment, an immense ocean which only the heart fathoms insofar as it overflows with faith, trust and love. There are no moments which are not filled with God's infinite holiness so that there are none we should not honour.*

There are many books written on mindfulness, increasingly so as we live lives which are too busy and suffer increased stress. A book I found well written and easy to read was by Ruby Wax[89]. Her experience, light and humorous touch are ideal if you are feeling stressed and need help in starting to train yourself in this practice.

Listening to ourselves gives greater peace and inner space to listen to others. We learn to take our own feelings more seriously and allow all our senses to be alive.

The act of reflection combines our listening of others, ourselves and God so that we are fully attentive to that which is going on around and within us.

*Eli said to Samuel, 'Go back and lie down. If the voice calls again, say "Speak, God. I'm your servant, ready to listen."'*[90]

# Mind Your Back

## Conflict

I don't think I have met anyone who likes conflict, but let's just clarify exactly what it is. Conflict is:

➢ to come into collision or disagreement; be contradictory, at variance, or in opposition; clash; be at loggerheads in everyday life.[91]
➢ and sometimes: to fight or contend; do battle as individuals and as communities/countries.[92]

Let's be honest – whilst we would love for this not to be the case, the reality is that conflict and disagreement is part of our everyday life.

Because I have been involved in the management of change in a business environment and also the institutional church, a leader is always going to encounter conflict when instigating change.

Jesus has this to say about conflict. Whilst his focus is on the group of people called 'church' it is equally applicable to business and personal situations:

*'If a fellow believer hurts you, go and tell him—work it out between the two of you. If he listens, you've made a friend. If he won't listen, take one or two others along so that the presence of witnesses will keep things honest, and try again. If he still won't listen, tell the church. If he won't listen to the church, you'll have to start over from scratch, confront him with the need for repentance, and offer again God's forgiving love.*

*Take this most seriously: A 'yes' on earth is 'yes' in heaven; a 'no' on earth is 'no' in heaven. What you say to one another is eternal. I mean this. When two of you get together on anything at all on earth and make a prayer of it, my Father in heaven goes into action. And when two or three of you are together because of me, you can be sure that I'll be there.*[93]

Those words are then followed in Jesus' next teaching where he says that we are to forgive our brother or sister seven times seventy. What he is saying is that the number of times we are to forgive should not be counted and that God has infinite forgiveness for us and that we are to be the same. Matthew, the writer, has gathered many of Jesus' teachings about dealing with sin, missing the mark and flaws within human beings. Using Jesus' teachings, what can we understand we need to do about times of conflict?

Sweeping situations of conflict under the carpet, ignoring it and wishing it would go away or burying our head in the sand is not in the mind of Christ. It needs to be dealt with head on for us and for those around us.

When I was leading a church internal reordering project to remove most pews and replace them with chairs, I encountered a few people who were very annoyed by what the church council and the institutional authorities had approved. We arrived at the approval by a long period of consultation and yet it was clear a very few people felt clearly threatened. Leadership means that 'the buck stops with you'. You are the people who receive the angry letters, emails and conversations. Emotional blackmail came into play as a couple of stalwarts of the congregation told me that if I took the pews out and replaced them with chairs, then they would leave and go to another church. I carefully listened, explained and although I felt threatened too, I had to say that I was sad to say the words, but I wished them every blessing as they moved to another church. A leader being threatened by a few people, when the greater number had approved, is not acceptable and the conflict has to be dealt with head on immediately.

It is right and wise to confront someone, or a small group, when they are by themselves and not in a public environment – as Jesus teaches. When you confront someone else's faults in front of others, it often humiliates them. No one likes to be humiliated, especially publicly, so it is good to deal with faults and imperfections during a one-to-one conversation.

Jesus' earlier teachings from the Sermon on the Mount tell us firmly that we are not to judge other people. He warns us about the difficulty of seeing the speck in another person's eye, when you and I have a log in our own eye. It is with a mood of humility and self-awareness that we approach another person whose fault is creating a conflict.

I've mentioned St Matthew gathering Jesus' teachings in chapter 18 of his Gospel, and when we read everything in context you realise that the heart of the church is to help each other to deal with each other's sinfulness. That task is very much for the leader/priest to take a lead role living out the mind of Christ. Of all gatherings, the church is a family which is to help each other with one another's imperfections, unhealthy patterns, and the way we sin against each other and ourselves. The church is to be a family that help's each other with individual and collective flaws. It is what families in our home life, and colleagues in our business environments should be doing too. We are to help each other to grow up and become mature people.

There is a danger in dealing with conflict, and meeting it head on, that individuals can become defensive and emotions can start to run high. Jesus reminds us that 'What you say to one another is eternal.' What we say to one another is received and can damage and hurt. The key action is to be patient and listen. The importance of listening to each other in conflict is true and right within marriages, parent-child relationships, at work and everyplace else where we have to deal with inevitable disagreements. There comes a time in all our lives when we actually need to listen to what others are saying about *our* shortcomings and flaws.

It is often easier in the short-term to sweep conflicts under the carpet and pretend they don't exist. The problem is that the damage it does is very unhealthy for everyone involved. It often destroys relationships and the issues often fester and cause mental health problems and sometimes affect our physical and spiritual health too. Trying to 'keep the lid on' conflict is sure to erupt at some point, when it then makes a terrible mess of lives that takes time to heal and move on.

A state of conflict existed with the Philippian Church, and St. Paul wrote out of his desire to see that conflict resolved. Any time people work together, tensions will develop. But unresolved tension brings reproach on the cause of Christ. Paul knew that this conflict could be resolved only if the Philippians had a change of heart – and a change of mind. The Christians had different minds; each one thought their own way. If Paul was to heal their divisions, he had to deal with their minds, reminding them that they were to have the mind of Christ, as we are too. He wrote:

*If you've gotten anything at all out of following Christ, if his love has made any difference in your life, if being in a community of the Spirit means anything to you, if you have a heart, if you care—then do me a favour: Agree with each other, love each other, be deep-spirited friends. Don't push your way to the front; don't sweet-talk your way to the top. Put yourself aside, and help others get ahead. Don't be obsessed with getting your own advantage. Forget yourselves long enough to lend a helping hand.*

*Think of yourselves the way Christ Jesus thought of himself. He had equal status with God but didn't think so much of himself that he had to cling to the advantages of that status no matter what. Not at all. When the time came, he set aside the privileges of deity and took on the status of a slave, became human! Having become human, he stayed human. It was an incredibly humbling process. He didn't claim special privileges. Instead, he lived a selfless, obedient life and then died a selfless, obedient death—and the worst kind of death at that—a crucifixion.*[94]

Whilst leading three churches I also took on the role of rural dean (in a way, equivalent to the role of an area manager). I had oversight of twenty-two churches and five other priests who were leading them. Recognising that with so much change happening we took almost three years of prayer, discussion, reflection and creative planning to find a new way in which these churches could operate and be led in the future. We consulted and listened to representatives of all the churches. All the priests agreed and I presented the plan to all the church councils, at one large evening meeting. A time was given to questions and comments, all of which were listened to, responded to, and made note of. There were three people who were rather aggressive in their comments and questions, all of whom came from a group of churches who may be split and join other groups. At the end of the meeting, I felt it would be right to approach these three people and listen more to their concerns. I didn't get an opportunity to say anything as a tirade of anger, followed by personal abuse was unleashed upon me, with many gathered around to listen. I remember feeling my fist clench and the anger rise within me. I felt it right to simply walk away without comment knowing that I could not trust any words I might say, or actions that I might take. Afterwards my colleagues made suitable murmurs of surprise and I asked the leader of those churches if they were going to do anything about it. The reply was simply 'That's what they are like.' I emailed my immediate superiors and just received a reply saying how sorry they were. For me, there was no concern and pastoral care. Nothing happened to heal the conflict, and sadly, through counselling, I realised that this was part of the crowning stress which manifested in my mental breakdown.

There is a report entitled *The Cracked Pot*[95] on the state of today's Anglican parish clergy, based on research during the period of 1996 and 2000. Sadly, so many of the issues identified remain, including this one mentioned in the section under internal conflict:

> *The clergy had a need to feel affirmed by the congregation but also the hierarchy. When this was not forthcoming, they felt hurt. This led to feelings of anger at the bishops, whom they felt did not accept the role of 'Father in God'.*

Conflict can manifest itself in many ways. A particularly damaging form is bullying. That applies to church leaders bullying their congregation as much as members of the congregation bullying their leader. The same applies in a business environment and also in the volunteer sector, including different styles of clubs. Everyone agrees – bullying is not acceptable in any form, but that is the same as saying that murder is not acceptable. The problem is that it happens and often, and very little is done about it. In fact, it is usually 'swept under the carpet'.

I have a good friend who I have known for many years. We have shared much and worked together on different projects. They have worked in the caring profession as well as the administrative structure of the church. They possess spiritual experience and knowledge, and lead a church as a parish priest. This person has encountered blatant bullying from selected members of the congregation because of their gender. Little was done in support from others around them – 'That's the way it is', 'That's the person they are' is no support to the person being victimised. I believe worse still is the lack of support from their senior church leaders on several individual issues. This manifested itself in rudeness to them, being oblivious and ignoring their need for pastoral support and even disgraceful behaviour to them at a rare face-to-face meeting. I so wish that I could say that this, and my own experience, is rare, but I am not just saddened, but horrified to say that it is not. Whilst I have no personal knowledge of church leaders bullying congregation members, I do have a deeply concerning experience of the number of clergy who have been bullied by their congregation, but more so by their colleagues and leaders. Writing policies on the issue has no value or respect unless those who are charged with implementing them apply them to themselves first and foremost.

For love in a time of conflict[96]


When the gentleness between you hardens
And you fall out of your belonging with each other,
May the depths you have reached hold you still.


When no true word can be said, or heard,
And you mirror each other in the script of hurt,
When even the silence has become raw and torn,
May you hear again an echo of your first music.


When the weave of affection starts to unravel
And the anger begins to sear the ground between you.
Before this weather of grief invites
The black seed of bitterness to find root,
May your souls come to kiss.


Now is the time for one of you to be gracious,
To allow a kindness beyond thought and hurt,
Reach out with sure hands
To take the chalice of your love,
And carry it carefully through this echoless waste
Until this winter pilgrimage leads you
Towards the gateway to spring.

# In Your Mind's Eye
## Vision

Proverbs 29: 18 is very direct: 'Where there is no vision, the people perish ...'[97]

The word perish in the Hebrew language (*para*) is accurately translated as to 'go back'. Paraphrased it reads, 'Where there is no vision, the people go back'. I dare to paraphrase myself by saying '... the people go backwards'.

A leader with no vision is purely a manager. I have heard over the years colleagues who are company directors, church leaders and members of bishops' senior staff team say that 'I'm just getting my head down and doing what I have to. That makes for an easier life.' This may be tough to hear, but if that is what you would say, then I don't believe that you are a leader. You are purely a manager. A manager who keeps the business running as it is, or a faith leader that is keeping the 'show on the road'. Anything for an easy life. Keeping the employees, the punters and the congregation happy. Some have also said, 'That way, everyone wins.' Wins at what? Being repetitive, being stagnant or stale, and, oh yes ... safe. Since when might you have read about the Trinitarian God being repetitive, stagnant, stale and safe? My experience of God is completely the opposite. Although God's character is unchanging, God actively desires us as individuals and as groups/churches of people to keep moving onwards. Essentially, we are a journeying people who are constantly being challenged to discern what to hold on to (what to repeat), and what to drop and pick up (to change and be new). Just because I am saying that vision is an essential part of being a leader in no way means that it is easy. It's tough. We are to actively move out of our comfort zone. Sir Francis Drake took a lead when he wrote this prayer:[98]

*Disturb us, Lord, when*
*We are too well pleased with ourselves,*
*When our dreams have come true*
*Because we have dreamed too little,*
*When we arrived safely*
*Because we sailed too close to the shore.*

*Disturb us, Lord, when*
*With the abundance of things we possess*
*We have lost our thirst*
*For the waters of life;*
*Having fallen in love with life,*
*We have ceased to dream of eternity*
*And in our efforts to build a new earth,*
*We have allowed our vision*
*Of the new Heaven to dim.*

*Disturb us, Lord, to dare more boldly,*
*To venture on wider seas*
*Where storms will show your mastery;*
*Where losing sight of land,*
*We shall find the stars.*
*We ask You to push back*
*The horizons of our hopes;*
*And to push into the future*
*In strength, courage, hope, and love.*

Asking God to disturb our comfortable life, to unsettle the way we do things, is seriously a challenging activity. However, Drake in the last line of his prayer speaks of strength, courage, hope and love. These are essential aspects of life in which to ground our disturbance.

Vision offers hope. Hope for the present and crucially for the future. St John (most likely) writing about a vision of heaven is crucial in Christian belief, that there is hope for everlasting life. The hope that life does not end when we die in our earthly body, but that our spiritual body is raised and we meet God, our creator, face to face. St Paul reminds us of this hope, writing to the Church in Corinth, saying, *'There are both heavenly bodies and earthly bodies ... It is sown a physical body, it is raised a spiritual body.'*[99]

It was an enormous privilege, as a church leader, to journey with people at the end of their earthly life, and to offer hope for the future. If families wanted me to choose which passage of the Bible to read and speak on at their loved one's funeral, I would always choose St John's vision of heaven written in the Book of Revelation:

*I saw Heaven and earth new-created. Gone the first Heaven, gone the first earth, gone the sea. I saw Holy Jerusalem, new-created, descending resplendent out of Heaven, as ready for God as a bride for her husband. I heard a voice thunder from the Throne: 'Look! Look! God has moved into the neighbourhood, making his home with men and women! They're his people, he's their God. He'll wipe every tear from their eyes. Death is gone for good – tears gone, crying gone, pain gone – all the first order of things gone.' The Enthroned continued, 'Look! I'm making everything new. Write it all down – each word dependable and accurate.'*[100]

St John, being bold enough to realise that his vision was important, writes it for all to read and hear. Literally, thank God for St John. This vision offers ground-breaking, awesome hope for all things to be made new. The 'first order' of a heavenly life, with all its weakness, sickness, pain, is to be spectacularly transformed into a sin-free life in a place called heaven, which is to far exceed our current understanding and expectations.

I specifically quoted the Message Bible paraphrase of St John's revelation because I firmly believe that it is not just for a life to come. Whilst I was at Hadleigh, I sat in my study with a good friend and colleague at the time, in what I called 'wasting time with God'. Taking some time to sit quietly, offering the time and space to God knowing that it would be honoured. In the silence I felt God nagging me to look at that passage from Revelation. I consistently ignored the nagging by saying to God that I knew the passage. I loved it, used it often and knew what it was about. The nagging persisted until I gave in with an audible 'All right!' I turned behind me to the book shelves and lay my hand on the first Bible available. The Message Bible. I read those verses and then read them aloud to my friend. I struggled to get the words out for shedding tears. My experience of God, when I shed tears in this way, means that God has something very important for me to hear, to know and act upon. God was tangibly present, so much so that I could touch Him. I heard God say that yes, he knew that I was aware of the hope this vision offered for the future, but it also offered hope right here, right now. I felt my jaw drop open and I was gobsmacked by God. This was a heavenly curveball that caught me unexpectedly in every way. Eugene Peterson's paraphrase using the words: 'God has moved into the neighbourhood, making his home with men and women! They're his people, he's their God,' overwhelmingly saying that he had moved into the neighbourhood of Hadleigh in a tangible way. Yes, God is present in every place, always without fail or specific reason, but this was God saying that he was present in a distinct way. From that time on, without people knowing about this, individuals would often say to me that when they entered St Mary's Church Hadleigh that they literally felt God's presence. God had moved in and was transforming things, a bit at a time, to that which was new. New and often unknown.

Vision and hope are very much linked. They are interlocking essentials for every leader, at whatever level, in whatever situation you find yourself. The thing is, that vision and hope are often crushed by cynicism. In business situations and also in church leadership there were definitely people who would say, behind my back, and sometimes to my face, that 'he's only doing all this new-fangled stuff to further his own gains'. What they mean is that the purpose of actioning vision and hope for the future was so that I would draw attention to myself and desire promotion in my job. Purposes were doubted and distrust niggled away inside a few people. Hope is spoiled by cynicism. I would even say that cynicism is the enemy of hope – it takes no courage to tear down radical vision.

I am aware that for many years I have been excited, motivated and inspired by the concept of vision and change. I thrive in a situation where someone provides a blank sheet of paper and requests some blue-sky thinking – thinking that is without boundaries and open to all the possibilities. In business we would take, at least once a year, a couple of days away from the office to formulate or update a strategic business plan. A plan shared with the owners and all employees detailing how the business was going to develop and grow. A key aspect was always how the products that we were selling were meeting the needs of customers. In the life of the Christian Church the process is similar. For several years I held the additional job role as rural dean (also known as area dean). It is the Church of England's equal in business to appointing an area manager with responsibilities for pastoral care of clergy and general oversight of churches in the area. Rural Deans met annually with senior bishop's staff to formulate a vision for the future. A flip chart list of changes was on display at the end of the time together and areas for action were agreed. When I moved from leading six rural churches in West Suffolk to the market town of Hadleigh, I took two years off the extra responsibilities of being rural dean. You always know that when the bishop invites you to lunch that there is 'no such thing as a free lunch'! I was persuaded to take up the extra job again and the next gathering of people was the annual meeting I spoke of earlier. I could hardly believe what I saw, when the list in front of us contained all the actions I had taken part of in formulating two years earlier! Having vision is excellent, but it is so important that the plan to enable the vision is actioned with clear times and responsibilities. Vision without action is fruitless and therefore pointless.

One of the ways to develop an action list is to formulate a Mission Action Plan. However, it is important to remember that mission is about what we do, it is not the vision itself. Mission is how we action the vision – formulating the steps so that we are on a journey to fulfil the vision. Taking as many people 'with you' on that journey is right and helpful. After a sabbatical I believed it was right to consult with as many people as I practically could to help me formulate a mission plan (an action plan) concerning the development of every area of church life. I've written more of this in the chapter on speaking and listening.

There are several people that we read about in the Bible who have dreams: God spoke to Israel in the visions of the night.[101] Pharaoh had a dream.[102] A vision appeared to Paul in the night.[103] In the book of Daniel we hear *'there is a God in heaven who reveals mysteries, and He has made known to King Nebuchadnezzar what will take place in the latter days. This was your dream and the visions in your mind while on your bed.'*[104] And there are more ... Solomon, Isaiah, Ezekiel, Amos to name a few.

Like many people, I dream. Very often I cannot remember what the dream was about when I wake up. Sometimes I remember and recall that it was a mismatch of people and things that I had recently thought about, together with some random fiction that makes no apparent sense. I had only been at Hadleigh a few weeks when one night I had a very clear dream. Before we moved into the deanery, I was decorating my study where the main window overlooks the churchyard and church porch. Sitting on the porch stone benches were a number of teenagers, and so, looking for an excuse to take a break from putting emulsion on the walls, I went out to sit with them and have a chat. I heard from them that the local youth club had been closed down and that there was nothing for them to do and the church porch was a place to meet up, especially in the winter or when it was raining. My dream clearly began as I saw the large wooden doors of the church opening and young people going in and out of the church. I could see that some had food and drink too. When I woke, I immediately told my wife, Pauline, what I had dreamed. It was such a clear and precise vision within a dream. I can't even remember thinking that I would simply 'park it' for the future, but instead I knew that God was not just asking me to do what I dreamed, but he was actively 'willing' it to happen. The Sunday service was only a couple of days away and very much planned. However, I knew that I needed to act on the dream and knew that we had to start a youth club within weeks.

When Anglican clergy look for new posts (jobs), they read the Parish Profile, which the church produces. It is a document that informs you about the places; what they do; the kind of person they are looking for; what the parish can offer you ... and so on. Hadleigh was clearly looking for someone to help them change to be a church of the future. I remember, as part of the interview process, making a presentation on collaborative (every member) ministry. It was based on the biblical account of Jesus feeding the five thousand.[105] That passage came flooding back to me as I thought about which Gospel Bible reading I was going to speak on concerning my dream. Music and readings were chosen, everyone informed and as I sat down to write my sermon, God clearly told me not to write it in advance – what I call winging it! God knows as well as I do that he has a better opportunity to speak clearly and directly if I have to put my total trust in him and pay attention as I stand to speak with no notes. My sermon recalled my dream, and related it to the Bible reading. I challenged the church to offer their physical, prayerful and financial help to start a youth club using the church building in two weeks' time. The church had no separate hall and it was very clear in my dream that it was the church doors opening.

Over the following days, I heard some people suck air though their teeth, sigh and shake their head. An air cynicism was born. But amazingly there were a few people who responded and both of my churchwardens gave their support. Little did anyone know how risky and costly this was all going to be. I named the youth club *The Porch Project* and on a Friday night, two weeks later, after telling young people that we saw, the church doors opened and we welcomed over twenty teenagers and provided food and drink. Over the years that followed the project developed into the largest youth project in Suffolk and we had over 750 young people on the register. Elsewhere in this book I have spoken about many aspects of this project, its amazing 'highs' and deeply challenging, sometimes 'lows'. What is important to say is that over time the church congregation and wider town and village community responded to this vision in a positive and often apprehensive way. All of this was entirely understandable – but 'thank you, everyone', because your action was integral to changing so many young people's lives. Thank you too, to the person who sent me this email which I recently discovered clearing out a filing cabinet:

*Dear Martin*

*Surely you know that, when you came to Hadleigh, and church members said they were relying on you to bring back the young people, they meant the well-behaved ones who would sit quietly in the pews while they were told how to worship and what to think and how things were done because that's how they'd always been done ...*

*We weren't expecting a priest who would have visions of a better way and expect us to do something to bring it about ...*

*My prayer is that your vision remains clear and unclouded and that you continue to challenge our complacency and our timorousness ...*

It was a couple of years after the project began that a close clergy colleague gave me a copy of this writing, headed 'The Dreamer' by Charles Peguy.[106]

*The Lord God said: I myself will dream a dream within you,*
*Good dreaming comes from me, you know.*
*My dreams seem impossible,*
*not too practical nor for the cautious man or woman;*
*a little risky sometimes,*
*a trifle brash perhaps.*
*Some of my friends prefer to rest more comfortably*
*in sounder sleep with visionless eyes.*
*But from those who share my dreams*
*I ask a little patience,*
*a little humour,*
*some small courage,*
*and a listening heart – I will do the rest.*
*Then they will risk and wonder at their daring;*
*run, and marvel at their speed;*
*build, and stand in awe*
*at the beauty of their building.*
*You will meet me often*
*as you work in your companions who share the risk,*
*in your friends who believe in you*
*enough to lend their own dreams,*
*their own hands,*
*their own hearts,*
*to your building.*
*In the people who will stand in your doorway,*
*stay awhile*
*And walk away knowing that they too can find a dream.*
*There will be sun-filled days*
*And sometimes a little rain –*
*a little variety both come from me.*
*So come now, be content.*
*It is my dream you dream,*

*my house you build,*
*my caring you witness;*
*my love you share*
*And this is the heart of the matter.*

Often, having the vision is the easy bit! As I have said earlier, it is how you put it into action. My dream and beginning *The Porch Project* happened very quickly. More often, visions take longer to come to fruition. If God is not being abundantly clear and direct, the leader needs to use all the 'tools in their box' to move things along. Discernment is a key aspect (written about elsewhere). I often shared ideas with a small number of people before making them public. People I respected who would pray, listen, reflect and be honest. It is crucial if you do this that you don't just choose 'yes people' – those who will just agree with everything you say, either because they don't want to upset you, or because they just want to be seen to hang out with the person who is leading. Sharing thoughts with at least one or two people who you know will challenge you in what you are saying. It helps you a great deal and develops your discernment skills and deepens your wisdom. Try not to share the complexities of a vision. Whilst you might have personally taken a great deal of time to think things through, those who you initially share with need to grasp the basic idea before the detail.

However crazy it might seem, stay faithful to the original vision. God is often bold and 'out of the box' (unlike most who want to keep him firmly in it!) If the vision doesn't scare you, then perhaps you are downgrading it and making it small. When you dream, when you do 'blue-sky thinking' too small, I believe you rob God of the opportunity to bring in a new heaven and a new earth – the beginnings of making all things new. Similar to St John, there are sometimes visions that we can share and begin to deliver, but we may not see the fruition. That may be for someone else to witness.

I have always been an advocate of change in leading businesses, but especially in the Christian church and particularly the Church of England. I believe that most denominations need to change drastically to effectively be the church that God has in mind for the time and culture in which we live. Sadly, I don't see any of them daring to catch a new vision, but rather a vision which is a tweak on that which already happens. In my most critical times I would say that the vision is just seeing a new way to rearrange the deckchairs on the *Titanic*. Most church attendance in denominations is going down at a pace. Changing the style of music, times of services, moving to the church hall, using trendy liturgy and all of that are not anywhere near the dynamic visionary change that is necessary. In my last two years of being rural dean, I attended a presentation by two members of the Church of England General Synod. They stated the obvious: church attendance is going down at a rapid pace and something has to happen. They based their presentation on five key words. I remember the three words which got me excited: prayerfully, urgently and dynamically. Finally, I thought, God gets the opportunity to begin something new (not tweaked) but new!

As part of our church's plan there were radical ways to change the governance and organisation of churches in my area. I brought through new ideas on inclusive acts of worship and more besides. I soon learned that when 'the rubber hits the road' and we actually start planning to act on the visionary ideas, that senior members of Church of England start backing off, being less supportive because it is getting rather uncomfortable as various church members start throwing their weight around and conflict is rife (see elsewhere). Emotional blackmail is always a card for church members to pull on their leaders. 'If you continue with this change, then I will ...' If we really say we want a new vision of church, do we really want it? Especially if it makes even us as leaders very uncomfortable and out of our comfort zone? If you dare to want God to show you a vision, don't expect an easy ride. But wow, when you witness it happen, make sure you thank God for the awesome privilege of being a part of it and being around to witness it.

My paraphrase of the proverb at the beginning of this chapter reads, *'Where there is no vision, the people go backwards.'* I have found myself in a few situations where I have been privileged to be part of a vision for the future. These visions have been collective in their ownership, but sadly when I have moved on to other things the clarity of vision has been lost and people have found themselves going backwards. Sometimes that is because it is risky, hard work and tiring, particularly enduring conflict from the few, and it is safer to just stop and revert to that which is familiar and ready-done. However, stopping the vision will never truly mean we go backwards. The journey so far will have already changed situations and people, so in many ways, although the vision is not fulfilled, the journey has not been a waste.

Speaking from personal experience, being a visionary is a hugely costly, sacrificial and risky aspect of being a leader in the mind of Christ. It is the way in which Christ led and leads through his leaders now. But let us all as leaders remember that 'Where there is no vision, the people perish...' Are you the stopper in the bottle of vision?

# Great Minds Think Alike
## Discernment

'I've got the opportunity to do this ... but I don't know if I should or not?'
'What am I supposed to do now that this has happened to me?'

Just two of the questions we often hear or ask ourselves. How *do* we know what to do? How do we know if we are making the right decision? Questions in our lives can be about very small issues, or they can be far greater life changing, or perhaps threatening ones – where to live; who to have a relationship with; what job to do, and so on.

Discernment is all about recognising or perceiving. It is a task in which our mind has a major part to play and if we have a faith, then we have the mind of Christ too. The combination, the coming together of our mind and the mind of Christ is powerful, especially when these two great minds think alike. How do we seek the mind of Christ? From my own experience there are many ways to go about this. I see them as 'tools in our box', every one of them at our disposal. Let me suggest what these tools are:

### Laying the issues before God

The reality is that God knows all that is going on in our lives and he knows us as individuals, completely. That doesn't mean to say that we can just sit about and do nothing, saying to God, 'You know what's going on for me, so I'll wait for you to tell me, or you can do just the right thing for me.' Believe me, it very seldom works like that! We are in relationship, in partnership with God. If we have a partner who we live with, and it is a decision that needs to be taken together, the right thing to do is to sit down with each other and talk about the options available. The same is true with God. Finding a quiet space and being conscious that God is present (even if it doesn't necessarily 'feel' like it) is a good place to start. In your own way, just talk to God, laying before him all that is on your mind. Be completely honest and leave nothing out. Talk through the facts but also share your emotions too. Finish by simply saying to God that you want to have his mind on the situation and say that you are open to receive what he has to say and do.

## Be practical – what are the facts?

When Pauline and I have needed to make decisions on where we were going to live, or what job to take, it is essential to sit down with the facts. It is really helpful to have lots of plain sheets of paper, or if you are really keen, larger flipchart paper and pens! Write down what the financial issues are. Are there any legal aspects to consider? Does the decision affect other people we care for and love?

Having two columns headed 'pros' and 'cons'. List what are the things that are 'for' making a possible decision, and what are those things which are against/negative/a concern.

Sometimes the tried and tested SWOT analysis is helpful. Four boxes, each with a different heading: Strengths, Weaknesses, Opportunities and Threats.

Don't forget that common sense is God given. Part of our discernment is to consider what simply seems common sense. Don't fall into the trap of being 'too heavenly minded that you are no earthly use'!

## Consult a council of saints

Sharing decision-making with others is a great way to tease out options and possibilities. I like the description of 'council of saints', because it is a about selecting one or more people who you perceive are wise in their faith with God and living out life in general. They are, if you like, saintly people.

I have been an instrument for change in much of my leadership life, both in business and the institutional church. Making right choices that affect the way in which others live and work is highly risky, and as much as possible, everything needs to be done to ensure that the decisions being made are as right as you are aware. The phrase 'taking people with you' is appropriate here. I would ask three or five people who I believe were wise and I respected. Asking those who you know who will just agree with you on everything is not at all helpful. Having a balance of those you know will listen to you, reflect back and also challenge you is, I have found, best. Speak to them individually, or together as a group. There also needs to be people who will respect confidentiality and respect that you are the person who will ultimately make the decision.

## Use all your senses

Perceiving the way to go is about using all our senses: hearing, seeing, touching, smelling, tasting. Sadly, I think people ignore these gifts. What are we hearing around us? What are we seeing? Did that touch from someone come at an important time? Perhaps less used are smell and taste, but hopefully you get the gist of what I am saying. Taking time to reflect on what is going on around us is important and helpful. Being present – being aware – of what is going on each day and living it in the knowledge that God is present, is part of being attentive for discernment. The future very often comes out of living in the present day and being attentive to it. We think that the real thing will happen tomorrow, later or at some other time. But the treasure of discernment is often hidden in the ground on which we are currently walking.

## Reading

Yes, of course, reading the Bible is a valid part of discernment. But, please be careful of how you do that. Opening the Bible at random, closing your eyes and pointing your finger to a sentence on the page isn't a helpful method. Neither is just looking at particular one-off verses or bits of the Bible that are well known to you. If you take part in a daily reading plan, continue with the plan and put what you read into the context of what is going on in your life. Someone who you are sharing your discernment with may suggest Bible passages. That can be helpful, particularly if they will listen to your reflections afterwards and continue the journey with you.

Reading other books, articles and so on can be helpful too, particularly again if they are written by those who are wise and respected, and are recommended by others.

## Waiting and patience

Historically I have a weakness: I'm impatient! Whilst in personality tests I am a 'reflector', I am also a 'doer'. If the balance is there on those two personality types, that is ideal. However, because of my impatience and desire to get on and make a difference, I can easily let the reflective side of me slip. I have been a person who has actively done things for others, rather than be content to allow others to do things to, and for, me. That balance is certainly restoring itself over the last few years.

When you have confidence, enabled by discernment, that you have a vision or prophetic picture, very often other people can't see or catch that same vision. However, it is essential that, with a gentle approach, you keep going and be faithful to God working things out for good.

Following the end of my time as a leader in the institutional church, a retired bishop shared in my discernment, with a particular focus on that which was spiritual. In my impatience I wanted to know what God wanted me to do next. Discerning that the answer was 'nothing at the moment', turned out it was about taking time to stop doing things to, and for, others, but allowing God and others to do things to, and for, me. That has been absolutely essential in my healing and wellbeing. The bishop recommended that I read a book called *The Stature of Waiting* by W H Vanstone. I had to get an old copy as it was out of print at the time. The back cover summarises the book well:

> *Certain puzzles in the Gospel Reports of the Passion of Jesus, are resolved when we see that the writers are presenting him as a waiting figure, and as one who, in his waiting, discloses the deepest dimension of the glory of God. This perception throws an entirely new light on those experiences of waiting and of dependence which, the writer believes, are becoming ever more frequent and widespread in contemporary life.*

The book is written from a wise, deep and spiritual place and for me was the right book to read at the right time. It turned my understanding of waiting from one of negativity to one of positivity. Associating with Jesus ministering in his time of waiting is incredibly powerful.

Times of waiting should not be seen as times of inactivity. Sitting back and doing nothing and expecting God to do everything isn't a relationship of partnership. The Christian seasons of Advent[107] and Lent[108] are about waiting, but waiting with activity and waiting with preparation. The word patience comes from the Latin verb *patior*, which means 'to suffer'. Waiting patiently is suffering through the present moment, sharing in it to the full, and letting the seeds that are sown in the ground of our mind develop into strong plants.

Times of waiting can feel barren and understandably difficult to navigate through, particularly if we think God is distant and quiet. I remember someone sharing a phrase with me that was so helpful. They said:

> When it says in the Book of Revelation[109] that there was silence in heaven for the space of half an hour, that was because God was moving the scenery for the next act.

Whilst we wait, God is not inactive. He is busy at work preparing that which is to come. Sometimes he prepares alone, other times he prepares with us (although we may not be consciously aware).

## Am I willing to take risks and trust?

When David Livingstone was in Africa, he received a letter. It said 'We want to send helpers. Have you found a good road into your area yet?' Livingstone wrote back, 'If they want to come when there's a good road, don't send them. I want people who'll come where there's no road.'

God has a habit of taking us out of our comfort zone. That immediately puts our reliance on him and not ourself − no bad thing! Out of offering ourselves to be available, God makes the impossible possible. We only have to look at the well-known story of the 5,000 hungry people.[110] Jesus told disciples, 'You give them something to eat.' It seemed impossible, but when they agreed they witnessed a miracle. God may lead us into seemingly impossible situations − don't avoid them. That's where we experience God. If you attempt only things you know are possible with the resources that you have, you'll receive the credit and God will have no part of it. When God performs the possible out of the impossible, the miracle happens. Then God will have the glory and we don't lose out − we receive great joy.

I spent twenty years working in one horticultural company, where I did the traditional thing of working my way through the ranks of the business ending in senior management. I was flattered a couple of times, being headhunted for other more senior roles in the same industry, but it never seemed the right time and one where I bottled out because it would involve moving to Canada. I trained as a priest in the Church of England whilst working full time in business and shortly after completing my final stage as a curate, I was headhunted again and this time accepted the role of Director of Horticulture. I knew that a key part of my role was to work with other members of the board of directors towards selling the family-owned company. After three years I said one day to my wife that I felt that my job was coming to an end, and sure enough a couple of days later I was made redundant. After agreeing a departure package, I returned home. After school finishing time our eldest son, then attending high school returned home. He saw my company car in the drive and thought this very unusual. I was normally much later home or often away on business. Pauline explained to him what had happened and immediately he replied, 'Oh well, he'll just be a full-time vicar now.' Nothing more was said and he went off to play with a friend as usual. Knowing that my generous salary, company car, health packages and mortgage were all about to change was unnerving to say the least. Discernment began and I was then selected for full-time priesthood. All the usual worries were taking place, but amazingly we paid the mortgage and all necessary bills, and had enough finances from my departure package to last until the very month I began to work in a set of six rural churches.

God often takes us out of our comfort zone, but he knows what he is doing and his timing is perfect. Always. John Henry Newman[111] said this:

*God has created me to do Him some definite service. He has committed some work to me which He has not committed to another. I have my mission. I may never know it in this life, but I shall be told it in the next. I am a link in a chain, a bond of connection between persons.*

*He has not created me for naught. I shall do good; I shall do His work. I shall be an angel of peace, a preacher of truth in my own place, while not intending it if I do but keep His commandments.*

*Therefore, I will trust Him, whatever I am, I can never be thrown away. If I am in sickness, my sickness may serve Him, in perplexity, my perplexity may serve Him. If I am in sorrow, my sorrow may serve Him. He does nothing in vain. He knows what He is about. He may take away my friends. He may throw me among strangers. He may make me feel desolate, make my spirits sink, hide my future from me. Still, He knows what He is about.*

## The origin of our thoughts

Is what we are thinking coming from our mind, the mind of Christ or somewhere else? I have always found the tool that Ignatius of Loyola offers in his Spiritual Exercises (written about earlier), to be of great help. He suggests that our thoughts are divided into two: Desolation and Consolation.

Desolation gives spiritual turbulence, that feeling of being churned up, uneasy. It often happens when we take our attention off God. We should ask ourself, honestly, are my thoughts and feelings driving me further away from God and developing my own self-interests and comfort? Persuasive thoughts that come from Satan are very much in this category, but do not think that all selfish feelings and thoughts are evil.

Consolation draws us closer to God. Surrendering to God and offering ourselves – who we are and who we are to become, is a great starting point. Our thoughts and feelings that lead us to a closer relationship with God are not to be ignored. We know that it is God because it has a freshness to it. Often it is better (or more radical!) than we could have thought ourselves.

## Prayer and reflection

I have not put this last because it is least important. Indeed, the list is not in any order of importance at all. The reason for putting this last is simply because it is the overarching 'tool' in the process of discernment. I have written more about this in a separate chapter. Part of living in the present with God is to be in conversation with him, in whatever way you find helpful. Times of reflection are essential in discernment. It is about setting aside a regular time, on our own, to replay the day or period since we last reflected. Looking for what I would call the 'ribbon of God'. What has been going on (when using some or all of the tools above), and what might now be connecting some of them? Where is the ribbon of God weaving through our daily life beginning to make things a bit clearer as to what his mind is about, and where might it start to connect to our mind? Where do these two great minds think alike?

# Mind Over Matter
## Taking good care of ourselves

This chapter is not intended to be a masterclass about how to look after ourselves. There are a vast number of books and other resources that will offer greater in-depth information. The content here is a reflection on my own life to date, and because I did not look after myself for a period of time, it resulted in the scary reality that I had experienced a mental breakdown that has taken over four years to recover from. You may already realise that you are not taking care of yourself, or know that something is not right within you. This is absolutely not the time to 'beat yourself up' about it, as that is likely to make matters worse. However, I believe that the concept of looking after ourselves begins with our mind, and that is where we need the mind of Christ to help us along. Hence the title of the chapter. The phrase 'mind over matter', in this context, means the ability to control problems, particularly how we feel, and especially when we are not well. Our mind is a very powerful 'tool', hence where we get the word willpower. Willpower has the ability to often triumph over material or physical experiences. The concept was written about by one of Rome's greatest poets, Virgil, who wrote the Latin epic poem *Aeneid* (*Mens agitat molem*[112], 'mind moves matter'), and later, in an entire system of philosophy, by Britain's Bishop George Berkeley[113], who believed that nothing in the world exists unless it is perceived by the human mind.

In the United Kingdom we live in the culture where many of us lead busy lives. Life lived 'full on' much of the time. We hear it, and say it often – 'I'm sorry I didn't do that but I'm so busy at the moment.' Periods of being busy are understandable and often necessary, but those periods should be short and manageable. There were definitely periods of time when I had roles in senior management, or when I was on the board of directors, when life was exceptionally busy. Long hours working, often away from home, were powered by passion, necessity and the prize of achievement. The same would be true during my time as a parish priest. There were times in the yearly Christian cycle which were busier than normal. It was in my final four or five years when being busy was normal. What went wrong during that time I have shared in the chapter 'Out of your mind'. Through counselling, I was brought to the reality that one reason for my breakdown, caused by burnout, was that I had very little self-worth. Over that period of about four years, I thought so little of myself that I was not taking good care of myself. I was so consumed by all that made up my 'work' as a priest, that I didn't matter. I have always been strong-willed and would just get on with the task before me, with no consideration for my own wellbeing or those closest to me. I think unconsciously I believed I was superman, or in this case, super-priest! How naïve and crazy that was. The danger of behaving in this way is that everyone (except those closest to you) think that you are okay and have your life under control.

Several years ago, at a conference in the bar one evening, I remember a parish priest, who had just been appointed as an archdeacon, sharing with a few of us that his parish never thanked him for what he did at the annual meeting. I thought very little about it, but if I am honest, I did wonder if perhaps he wasn't doing a very good job, and consequently wasn't thanked. That was until the last four years as a licensed priest in the Church of England, when one of my churches, the largest out of thirteen that I had been priest to over the years, didn't thank me at the annual meeting either. I even heard someone in a senior leadership role in my church say to someone (obviously thinking I was out of their hearing) that they didn't tell me how good a job I was doing as I might get a big head. I even tried to explain to myself that the year-on-year occurrence was down to the fact that God called me to sacrificial ministry, and that I wasn't doing it for reward. When talking through those years I realised that I had increasingly felt that I didn't matter. On the other hand, if the church leader doesn't thank everyone by name and the role they play, at the annual meeting, or thank people after what they do at shared meals, or putting on a fete (and so on), they will be in deep trouble. The same applies to managers and directors in a business environment. But who is thanking them for what they do, on a regular basis? It is far from making big-heads, but rather acknowledging who they are and what they do, to build them up and encourage them.

When looking for a new job, in whatever environment, the applicant is most often informed as to the type of person that is being sought after. This usually includes what skills and experience is required. This would be true when churches are seeking a new leader, they will describe what is currently going on and some will describe their aspirations, challenges etc. for the future. This is what they want the applicant to do for them. Very often, but only in recent years, they will list what they can do for the applicant. This is usually a shorter list! My experience of being on both sides – as an applicant and employer or interviewer, is that what the organisation can do for the applicant is quickly forgotten. However, there are good examples of businesses and churches caring for their leaders and workers. In my earlier years some churches would often ask me 'how are you?'; sometimes they would collectively give me and the family a gift at Christmas to express their gratitude. Occasionally a box of homemade cakes would appear on the doorstep, or in season a brace of pheasants! Sadly, in my final seven years as parish priest there appeared to be a lack of tangible care. I suspect this was something to do with the grand title which I was given, and there was often an attitude of 'why do we need to do that, that is what he is paid to do'. The understanding of being in church and the call to be collective in ministry was overshadowed by expecting those who were staff to do everything, whilst the remainder turned up to be 'done to'. Thank God, literally, for some individuals and one of the rural churches that bucked that trend.

The reason for sharing all of this is because leaders need to have self-worth as the foundation to building the bricks of taking good care of oneself. Knowing that those who you work with, and for, appreciate you, love you, respect you, and value you is so important. The leader cannot look after others if the others are not looking after the leader. This creates a healthy mindset. With the mind of Christ we are reminded that, as individuals, we are worthy of taking care of ourselves because that is what God wants us to do. We are God's children who he loves and cares passionately about, and that is to be worked out through other people as well as ourselves.

Leaders who do not feel loved, valued and have self-worth will struggle to take good care of themselves, and that is where the spiral of decline begins. Having a mind that is consumed by what has to be done, and what other people need, takes over, sometimes because it is safer to stay in the familiar place of doing for others than caring for oneself. Over a period of time leaders become disillusioned, unmotivated and often encounter difficulties in relationships within the working environment, and also on a personal basis. This is why it is so important to have trusted people to talk to; a small number of people who act as a network support group; together with close family members.

When we are stressed, overworked, tired and unappreciated the thought of looking after ourselves seems too large a task to undertake. How can we take more exercise, or spend more time socially with others, if we just don't have the time? This is where having mind over matter is so important. Having the mind of Christ enables a healthy mind, to say that 'I am worth it', 'I am important', 'I deserve to look after myself'.

Working from a base that there are three areas of ourselves which need to be looked after – these being our body, our mind, and our spirit. These aspects of our very being are interlinked. When one part is not healthy it very often affects one or the other parts. If we are physically unwell our mind and our spirit are affected too. This is why a holistic approach to looking after ourselves is so important. I should say that when I am talking about spirit, in this context, it is not necessarily about being expressed as faith or religion.

Stress can be a key reason as to why we don't look after ourselves. I don't mean occasional stress, but rather prolonged and excessive stress. I tried to relieve my excessive stress by drinking alcohol at the end of each day. At the peak it would be a bottle of red wine per day, plus beer and spirits at the weekend. I learned in hindsight that this affected my sex drive, my sleep patterns were destroyed and as a consequence I slept less hours than I needed. The alcohol made my concentration at the beginning of the morning poor, and there were times when I led a communion service at 8am on Sunday morning nursing a hangover headache. I still drink alcohol, but it is because I enjoy it for its taste, rather than for its effect. That effect is often as a relaxing agent which leads to helping to forget what is stressful. Having loved ones who keep an eye when drinking is excessive is helpful, provided that they do it in a constructive, caring and compassionate manner.

Getting enough sleep is essential to our wellbeing. Some of us may need slightly more or slightly less than the average prescribed seven to nine hours. Human sleep is accompanied by complex changes that occur in the brain – they help to 'file things' in the appropriate area of the brain, clear away unimportant thoughts and a great deal more. Hence quality sleep is so important.

Regular exercise is always good, alongside what we eat and drink, to keep us healthy. For many years I used to play badminton. Team sport and sport with others is equally important, for the social aspects and a natural environment where all round pastoral care can take place. Time to meet with friends and family around the dinner table, play games, go to the pub or for a walk (or both!) means that we are active in the old saying 'a change is as good as a rest'. Environments where we can have fun and laugh are great healers. Taking time to 'chill out' and relax and be conscious of what our body is telling us enables us to be in tune with what we need to do, or not do, for healthy living.

Being aware of who we are as a person helps with what is right for us to be doing in taking good care of ourselves. I am naturally an introvert who reflects a great deal. People used to say, 'Why doesn't Martin talk much during meetings? But then, when he does talk it is worth hearing.' I tend to listen carefully at meetings before making a considered response. Being an introvert, I am absolutely not the 'life and soul of the party'. I am much happier to spend time with those I know and not be forced into situations where I have to do small-talk. When we are forced to act out of genuine character, a greater level of stress is added to any already present. This can be an aspect of compassion fatigue – often a holistic exhaustion of listening to, and caring for those who are sick or traumatised, over an extended period of time. Whilst saying that, I loved, and still love, spending time with people to listen and help, when and where I can.

If you are a creative kind of person: painting, drawing, photography, crafts etc., then giving yourself permission to take time to do that helps to rest tired areas of our brain and do something more practical that requires very little thinking. Hobbies are very much part of this too, whatever yours might be.

Keeping our mind stimulated intellectually keeps our wisdom and knowledge developing. Reading fiction books helps our mind to be led into a completely different context to our regular life. Non-fiction books, particularly those connected with our personal and social interests, help us to switch off work and life mode and learn new things. Attending short courses to learn language, cooking and so on reinforce the fact that 'I am worth it' and 'I deserve to do this'.

Setting personal and family goals enables us to have things to look forward to. Ensuring at the beginning of the year that holidays are booked as a priority, as well as key social times: concerts, shows, children's key events etc., helps in keeping the right work-life balance. In earlier years I used to use the tip someone gave me, which was to write off evenings or afternoons, or whenever with nothing planned. Writing in the diary 'something' across the chosen period of time, means that when someone asks if you are available then, you can honestly reply, 'I'm sorry, I have something already in the diary.' If you are working well and doing a good job, and putting the right hours in, then you absolutely deserve to take time out. You are worth it! This comes into the area concerning boundaries. Over the last seven years in the institutional church, I was absolutely useless at putting boundaries in place. Boundaries are about time management: getting the work-life balance planned in the diary and sticking to it. When my wife reads this, she will roll her eyes and say to herself 'if only he had'. Not just learning to say the word 'no' but actually using it is vital. Learning to say to people who hang to you like a leech sometimes, 'I'm sorry but I have something else to go to now,' takes you away from energy sapping people and situations. This must always be done sensitively.

When I was seeing a psychiatrist, and after his diagnosis, he said to me that the first thing I needed to do was to take control. There were definitely times when I was a control freak, didn't delegate or was obsessed with doing something because I didn't trust that others could do as good a job as me. But he meant that I needed to take control of me. In fact, I needed to take back control of me. For too many years I had allowed other people to be, I suspect unconsciously, in control of my life. This is back to boundaries – I was the one who had not put the boundaries in, or if I had, I had ignored them. Giving myself back self-worth and saying 'I am worth it' put me back in control of my life. That was not easy at first, as being a trained theologist[114], my old evangelical roots kept saying that God was in charge, not me. That latter view is deeply unhelpful and damaging, as I know for myself and for others that we are in a relationship of love and partnership with God, not a hierarchical situation where God moves us around like a piece in a chess game.

I've written quite a lot in other chapters about spiritual rest and refreshment, including mindfulness. However, before I finish this chapter, I want to include health professionals. One thing I have been good at is regularly asking my doctor to carry out a 'body MOT', otherwise known as a well-man check-up. It is a time when the doctor carries out a set number of checks to make sure that there is nothing health-wise lurking in your body that may need later attention. I have found that check-up helpful to address anything needed quickly and also rest your mind that there isn't a surprise waiting to catch you out. I've spoken in another chapter about talking and listening, but my experience, and sadly many others, is that most institutions (church our otherwise) are not good at professional caring. There is often a distinct lack of trust and experience and so I would always suggest getting external qualified help in all the three areas of body, mind and spirit.

Complementary therapies should not be ignored. When I formed a healing ministry team in the six rural churches I was leading, we offered massage. Receiving a physical massage when someone who is praying for you as they do it is deeply powerful. In fact, I would go myself on a regular basis. There is quite a list of complementary therapies, most of which are compatible with faith, but make sure you check beforehand what you are happy with.

The reality is that we are all people who are living and working with wounds. Open wounds of things currently going on, as well as scars of previous times. Allowing our open wounds to fester, and developing stress with a desire to have our own way, even though it may not be the best for us, is a dangerous position to be in. We have to stop trying to live life against itself and against what God desires for us, because we are loved and worth it. We are to stop being driven, and take control again by getting back in the driving seat, driving with God.

# Spring To Mind
## Transformation and restoration

When someone asks me what God is all about, the overarching aspects of his character which spring to mind are transformation and restoration. When life is tough, seemingly hopeless and we believe it is heading in a direction we would prefer not to be part of, it is life giving for us to 'spring to mind' that God has the power to change it. That doesn't necessarily mean changing our life to make everything brilliant at the time and in the way we prefer. Oh no!

There is a false belief held by so many people: God is unchanging and therefore he does not do anything in our lives that instruments the work of change. Balderdash!

Let's establish a firm foundation: God is unchanging in who he is (I still use the word 'he' although, for me, God is beyond gender). James, in his first letter confirms

*Every good and perfect gift is from above, coming down from the Father of the heavenly lights, who does not change.*[115]

God speaking to Malachi is direct in saying:

*I the Lord do not change ...*[116]

If this is true of God, then it is true of Jesus. The writer of the letter to the Hebrews says:

*Jesus Christ is the same yesterday, today and forever.*[117]

Our understanding is that God is manifest in three persons: Father, Son and Holy Spirit. All three are unchanging in who they are. So, it is with this foundation built that we can ask 'what is God all about?' Whether you have read the Bible from cover to cover, read bits of it, heard Jesus' parables or whatever, for me, looking at the wider picture, everything ends up being God's work of transformation and restoration. God may go about that work in a vast array of ways, over differing lengths of time, but it is always the purpose. God wants, desires, that the people he created change – change to be more Christlike. Why? Simply because he loves us unconditionally and wants what is right for us. That will be different for every one of us.

One of the most awesome works of God's ability to transform and restore, is Jesus' resurrection. The first time I saw Mark Cazelet's painting in Chelmsford Cathedral, I was mesmerized. Entitled *The Tree of Life*, it is dominated by an oak tree, with St Cedd[118] sitting to the right, under the tree. Above, the tree is alive and surrounded by golden corn. On the left, the tree is dying and surrounded by environmental degradation. Look carefully and you will see a skeleton hanging with thirty pieces of silver falling from his hand. This is Judas Iscariot, who was instrumental in Jesus' arrest leading to his crucifixion. Look high up on the right side again and peeping in between the lush growth and the flowers is a person, wearing the number 12 on his t-shirt. This is Judas Iscariot enjoying the tree that brings life. On first view, the discovery of Judas there had me in tears. Any of us to presume that Judas is beyond forgiveness by God for what he did is wrong. The transformative and restorative work of God is beyond measure and human understanding. The unconditional love of God is exactly that. It is absolutely not for us to judge and assume who or how God works in and through. What we must believe and have hope in, is that God is more than capable of doing all of this for and in us.

I preached an Easter Day sermon based on that painting and witnessed God working in people's lives as they listened and as they shared with me after the service and the days that followed. The resurrection of Jesus from death is the most powerful of all reality, showing us that God has the power to work beyond our imagination.

Simply doing good works, being a good person is a great thing to do, but what we 'do' comes out of who we 'are'. If we 'are' transformed by God, then what we do is empowered. Dennis Kinlaw writes:

*God calls us beyond merely 'doing right'. He calls us to be people who live in his way because we have his own heart. He calls us to be changed into his righteous people by the transforming power of his Holy Spirit. Right living results from the transformation of a person's mind and heart, rather than from any kind of self-imposed discipline.[119]*

I am reminded of that saying that 'we are to be in the world, but not of the world'. It is based on Saint John's writings, when he records the prayer which Jesus makes to God the Father for his disciples, before his crucifixion:

*I gave them your word; The godless world hated them because of it, because they didn't join the world's ways, just as I didn't join the world's ways ... I'm not asking that you take them out of the world, but that you guard them from the Evil One. They are no more defined by the world. Make them holy – consecrated – with the truth ...[120]*

Our task, our mission if you like, is to get on with living in the world but to be different. Paul, writing to the Romans says:

*Do not conform any longer to the pattern of this world, but be transformed by the renewing of your mind. Then you will be able to test and approve what God's will is – his good, pleasing and perfect will.[121]*

When our minds are transformed, we become incredible partners with God in the world. We are contributors to what God is doing, not just robots. This relationship is not one of employer-employee interaction. Jesus says that we are not a servant either, but rather a friend.[122] Saint Paul describes the relationship as even closer and intense describing it as a co-heir:

*... we are children of God, and if children, then heirs, heirs of God and joint heirs with Christ – if, in fact, we suffer with him so that we may also be glorified with him.[123]*

In creation we see this kind of partnership. God creates animals and Adam names them. We live and work together with God, not for God.

Suffering is something that I am not aware anyone desires, if we are truly honest. Living a transformed life with the knowledge that we have the mind of Christ means taking the rough with the smooth; the good with the bad; the life-sapping with the life giving. Whatever our suffering, and at whatever level we encounter it is crucial to our life journey. At the time of writing this chapter the United Kingdom has encountered a serious health pandemic in the form of COVID-19. Everyone has been affected in some kind of way that has made a difference to the way we live out our daily lives. It has gone on for a great deal of time and understandably I hear people long for the situation 'to get back to how it used to be'. That can't ever be the case. We want things to be restored to how they were before we were affected. God's work of restoration doesn't do that either.

Pauline, my wife, and I have always bought houses that needed work doing to them. We often say that we buy dumps and do them up! Sometimes we have said that we restore the house and we hear frequently that historic houses undergo restoration. What that really means is that the essence of the house is restored – much of the original features are brought back to good condition, and so on. It doesn't mean that if it is a Victorian House that there will be no central heating and double glazing. The restoration is completed with the knowledge of things discovered and learned and blended together. When we encounter suffering, hardship, trauma, our life is changed for ever. When life becomes easier it can never return to how it was before, simply because we will live life in the knowledge of what has happened to us.

God's work of restoration brings us first and foremost back in tune with God's desire for creation. For humankind to be in relationship with himself. The most well-known Psalm of all, twenty-three reminds us as the psalmist says '… he restores my soul.'[124] God brings us back to himself, he restores our very being to be close to his.

Living with the wounds of difficult, traumatic and devastating times in our lives leaves scars. I have led retreats and spoken often about the reality of being wounded. I have used the visual aid of a glass:

My sister, knowing that I love the occasional drink of whisky, bought for my birthday (many years ago) a pair of cut-glass whisky tumblers. It was only a year or so after, in the process of washing one up, I placed it into water which was too hot. The glass instantly cracked clean in half. I was devastated. I didn't know what to do. I desperately wanted to fix it, partly because I loved what it looked like, and partly because I was scared as to what my sister might say! I dried the glass, waited a while then got some superglue and put the two pieces back together. I placed the glass, next to the other one, in the glass cabinet, which was on view to anyone who came to the house. Having turned the glass around, the crack was not visible to anyone. The only other person who knew was my wife.

Our broken lives are so often treated the same way as my broken glass. We want to hide it or instantly fix it and put it back to the way that it was. We want to retore it. But the reality is that the glass, and our lives, cannot ever be the same again. The crack of the glass, the scar of our trauma (or whatever) will always be there. The question to reflect on, is 'How visible is our brokenness and our scars?' Do we allow them to be visible and heard, or do we hide them away, just as the way I turned the glass around on display so that the crack was hidden from view? God restores our lives but asks us to acknowledge and display our brokenness so that other people's lives may be transformed and restored too. After Jesus' resurrection, as he appears to the disciples, he shows them his scars of crucifixion – his sign of humanity and the reality of the struggle. By doing so, lives are changed and empowered.

We cannot demand from God that our lives will be trouble free – not this side of heaven. It is about living the reality of the struggle between what God accomplished by Jesus' death and resurrection and the time when Jesus comes again. Jordan Peterson[125], in an article which appeared in a well-known Sunday magazine, wrote an item headed 'Even in the maelstrom of modern life, the lessons of Easter can't be ignored'. He finishes with this paragraph:

> It is necessary for each of us to open ourselves up to the tragedy of being. It is psychologically true that we should encounter Satan in the desert, understand ourselves as the epicentre of evil as well as good, pick up our tragic burdens and crosses, die, and renew our souls.

*That is the death and resurrection, celebrated by Easter, and it is time for us to wake up and recognise it as such.*

That renewal is about transformation and restoration which, like it or not, brings change in our life, and potentially others too. The preference that we want God to do new things through us but in familiar ways is not on God's agenda!

Whilst I was working my way through a massive time of trauma through stress in my life, which led to disastrous consequences, I received a card from someone I had never met but had heard of me over a number of years and what I was going through. The card, handwritten said:

*When the bough of the apple tree is overloaded with fruit, it will sag and stoop down to touch the earth. I pray most earnestly that the abundant love of our creator will surround and protect you, while he raises you up into the new life which awaits you.*

The sending of that card at such a time helped me to spring to mind all that God promises. He was, and continues to be, truly faithful to that promise.

# Mind Your Language
## Authority, confidence and language

One of the characteristics of being a leader is to receive authority. In human terms this may be determined as a lot or just a little. Little or great, it is still authority. And authority is powerful. Done well, it can make changes and a difference for good. The words associated with authority certainly give the impression of power: enforcement; official permission; give orders; make decisions; sanction; organise; commanding; influence; in charge; the right to ...; obey. I am sure there are more. It is when authority misuses power that potential damage, in a range of ways, can be encountered.

Authority executed well relies on our mind interpreting and executing the responsibility, but having the mind of Christ turns the worldly understanding of authority on its head. Jesus, being fully human and fully God, has authority – the authority of God the Father, the creator of all things and people. Justin Welby, Archbishop of Canterbury says

> Jesus does not deny that he has power and authority, though he has not sought that power for power's sake. His power comes from being faithful to the will of his Father. He is absolutely certain about his mission and his calling. As the opening verses of John 13 say, he knows from whom he has come, what he has to do and where he is going. He rests in the assurance of being one with the Father, utterly at the centre of the will of God... He does something that no one expects or anticipates. Jesus subverts the whole notion of power and leadership, by taking the role of a servant... True power lies in washing feet, in taking up the role of a servant.[126]

You see what I mean about Jesus turning worldly authority upside down? True authority involves serving others, and power is the ability to sacrifice yourself. It is less about a hierarchical approach (the person at the top with the greatest amount of authority telling everyone else what to do), but more about a level playing field. I use that description simply because it is like a football team where all the players are on the field, but there is someone appointed to be the captain. Jesus is very much a team player and it is from this stance that he executes authority. In both leading businesses and churches, I was part of a team of people who I worked with, and for. Sometimes that meant I got involved in helping others (seeming less experienced than me) in what they were doing. There were times when I had to exercise authority, but it was always from within the work team, or through congregational members.

Another aspect of Jesus' style of authority is that it is influential. In other words, it is an authority that has the capacity to have an effect on people's character, their behaviour and personal growth. One of the times where Jesus executes this is when he rests at Jacob's well and meets the Samaritan woman who comes to draw water.[127] Jesus does not claim how important he is when the woman asks if he is greater than their ancestor Jacob. By simply talking about water, he demonstrates the difference between Jacob and himself. His authority is firm when he knows that she has five husbands. The woman realises that Jesus is a prophet, not by his being dictatorial, but rather meeting her on a level, as a team player, but one who is gentle but firm about the truth. Jesus is influential in her life, so much so that her life will be changed by the encounter.

The team model of authority works! Yet I have worked with two Anglican bishops who freely admitted that often they adopted a 'bottom-up' style. I know I said that Jesus turns our understanding of authority upside down, but I did not mean it literally in this sense. 'Bottom-up' authority and management are where everyone, supposedly under authority, determines many of the decisions themselves and simply get on with whatever, informing the main leader. My experience of many years of this was that there was no common oversight, vision and direction, resulting in little respect but a great deal of frustration. The team, including the captain, need the manager, who is detached yet part of the whole, providing clear direction, oversight and care. In this crude example, I see Jesus as the captain, playing with us, but God is in overall charge. In the Anglican Church, the bishop plays the role of 'Father in God' whilst individual clergy are captains of the local team. In a business model, managers are captains with the board of directors in overall charge.

It would be a reasonable question to ask where our authority comes from. For me, I agree with many who say that authority comes in two ways:

Conferred authority – This is the authority that is bestowed on us. It is given to us by the role that we undertake. For example, a business giving authority to a manager; the institutional church giving authority to a bishop or parish priest. In terms of faith, it is also the authority which is given by God at baptism.

Derived authority – Made up, in part, as a reflection of our character, who we are as a person. It is about our ability to make relationships, what we have to offer by our life experience and wisdom.

Having the mind of Christ in our authority means that we have a balance of both conferred and derived authority. Sometimes, depending on when and what we are doing, the balance will tip either way, but should contain aspects of both. Overall, our authority to be who we were created to be, and act as God desires, is given, in fact gifted, through Jesus to us. Jesus says to the disciples, and therefore to us:

*Jesus came and said to them, 'All authority in heaven and on earth has been given to me. Go therefore and make disciples of all nations, baptizing them in the name of the Father and of the Son and of the Holy Spirit, and teaching them to obey everything that I have commanded you. And remember, I am with you always, to the end of the age.'[128]*

This conferred authority, for us as disciples, is to be merged with derived authority from our own lives, resulting in achieving great things for God. Jesus asks us to trust him but also challenges us:

*Believe me: I am in my Father and my Father is in me. If you can't believe that, believe what you see—these works. The person who trusts me will not only do what I'm doing but even greater things, because I, on my way to the Father, am giving you the same work to do that I've been doing. You can count on it. From now on, whatever you request along the lines of who I am and what I am doing, I'll do it. That's how the Father will be seen for who he is in the Son. I mean it. Whatever you request in this way, I'll do.[129]*

Receiving this authority and acting on it has to be done with confidence. Confidence in who we are as children of God; in the role in which we are called to play in life and organisations by our commissioning; confidence in all that we gain as wisdom and knowledge; confidence in our relationship with God as loved and forgiven unconditionally; confidence in what we have done, and are as a person (warts 'n all). I have observed over recent years that confidence can manifest itself in two wrong, and therefore unhealthy ways. First, in the form of arrogance, by being so cocky about things that people turn away. And second in the form of being wishy-washy: being almost scared to say anything with confidence for fear of not being politically correct, or afraid of what people might think of us. Neither of these extremes of confidence is honouring to God, ourselves, and those who we work with, or serve. It often alienates and stifles growth and development, and is a sure way to lose co-workers and friends.

Our conferred and derived authority is worked out in what we do and what we say.

Finally, in this chapter I want to share a little of my current frustration, particularly with the Christian Church (in most denominations) about the way it uses language. For those of us who have been in 'the club' of the church for many years, the use of Bible sentences, prewritten liturgy for services of worship and listening to someone preach is, mostly, understandable. However, those club members are declining rapidly. Some love the poetical language in the Book of Common Prayer and the King James Bible. Some prefer the rewrite in other Bible translations and worship books such as Common Worship. These are just a couple of examples. Some even like to say the familiar words because they sound good and make them feel comfortable, as though they are back 'in the old days', but don't have real understanding as to what they are really saying! I think the greatest 'no-no' for me is churches and people putting up posters, or speaking, quoting one or two Bible verses. These quotes are used in the context of wanting to grow the church or encouraging people to think about God, and yet the majority of people read or glance at them and swiftly forget because they have no idea what it is saying. I believe the church is beyond confident to the point of arrogance, that just because it believes in God everything they say is right, and everyone else is wrong and a sinner. Little wonder the institutional church is in decline, either because people are not attracted by what they see and hear, so don't join, or are leaving because the church is so disconnected from the culture in which we live, and the way in which people desire to live out their faith. When is the institution going to put itself in the shoes of 'others outside the club' so that it can meet them where they are in terms of place and language, just as Jesus did? Yes, club members are important, but the focus is well beyond balanced at the moment. More about this in the chapter on the Church.

# Minding Out For One Another

## Compassion and pastoral care

It would be true to say that we all want to be cared for, in some kind of way. Caring in this sense is about minding out for someone; being concerned for them; to look out for and look after. Caring is almost always a very practical act. It takes the thought in our mind of wanting or being prompted to care, and turns it into that which is tangible – real.

Linked very closely with caring is compassion, because compassion is also about the act of 'doing' and particularly about 'entering into'. I often hear the word compassionate used in the sense of someone being thoughtful and perhaps understanding of someone's need, and certainly those are elements of what it is to be compassionate. However, it is a great deal more than that, as it is about connecting to, and sharing with, the suffering of another person. It is far from passive, but rather a deep and costly act, and is a movement to true empathy, which is feeling as another by entering into the need with care. That level of activity leads to a motivated desire to help prevent or alleviate suffering. This can seem a massive task, but Paul Gilbert, a professor and Buddhist meditator and teacher, and his co-writer Coden, also a teacher, say this:

*Compassion is not about being overwhelmed or sinking into our own or other people's pain; it is not about being superficially nice so people will like us; it is not weakness, softness or letting people off the hook if they are harmful. The key to compassion is tuning into the nature of suffering, to understand it in the depths of our being and to see clearly into its source; but equally important is to be committed to relieve it and to rejoice in the possibility of the alleviation of suffering for all.[130]*

113

Making every attempt to be compassionate to someone and wanting their suffering to be made better, or taken away cannot necessarily be achieved by you or I alone. I've said before that so many times I have wanted to do everything I could to make that possible, so that I could, figuratively speaking, put a bandage or plaster on the problem, pat the person on the head, and say 'everything will be all right now'. We do need to do everything that we possibly can, ranging from practical help to listening, but we may be one of a few people doing different things to help.

Only three months into a new post to lead three churches, I had a phone call one Sunday afternoon to say someone delivering church magazines had been seriously hurt in a hit and run accident. I immediately went to the scene where the emergency services, including the air ambulance, were present and I watched them closely doing all that they could. After quite a long period of time, when the air ambulance took him to a trauma hospital in London, I went with a police officer to break the news to his family. A few days later I travelled to the centre of London to visit him, where holding his hand and saying a few words were all that I could do as he laid in a coma. It was a considerable time, due to the permanent damage to his health, before he was returned to be cared for near his home town, and his family visited regularly for several years until his death. Whilst I entered into all of that with compassion, sadly I could never make the situation miraculously change. Professional carers in the widest sense can only do 'what they can do' by being available and loving through caring.

Over twenty years I have conducted hundreds of funerals. I have also been to many funerals as a mourner too. I believe there is a difference in someone leading a funeral who has been detached from the family, and leading as part of their job, and one who has entered into the situation with compassion and empathy. Leading a funeral on behalf of the deceased family takes time and desire. A desire to truly listen with care, be interested, and allow the family to share their feelings as they talk through the life of the person who has died. Leading a funeral is far from going through the motions of what a leader, pastor or priest ought to do, but rather acknowledge that it is a vicarious role that is to be executed. It is where the Church of England gets its word/role of vicar. Vicarious, meaning to do something on behalf of someone/some others. In this case, it is never to be about 'us', but always to be about others.

Within the period of 18 months, I found myself walking alongside and leading the funerals for three separate families whose loved one had taken their own life. It took a great deal of physical time, especially where the deceased had young children. It is equally demanding to lead a funeral for a baby, young child or teenager. It matters not how many times you do that, if you are doing it with compassion then it will be costly. I am referring to this cost particularly when you are part of the caring profession. The same will be true if you are alongside an individual and their family, whilst someone is in the last stages of their earthly life. The privilege is great if you witness their death, but also emotionally and spiritually draining. I have also sat with teenagers in church buildings who were self-harming. This is why it is so important to have people around you who you can talk to, not just at set times, but will be there at the time you most need. I wrote about this in the chapter about speaking and listening.

Wanting to alleviate pain without sharing it is like wanting to save a child from a burning house without the risk of being hurt ourself. When we do not run away from others' pain, but touch it with compassion, we take part in the process of healing with solidarity. However, this requires a careful balance of entering into someone's pain, walking alongside them, helping in whatever ways are possible, but not being overwhelmed and sinking into their pain. The task of taking on another's pain is done by Jesus Christ alone. As Jesus goes through his arrest, praying in the Garden of Gethsemane, his trial, walking to the place of his death and hanging on the cross,[131] so he is the one and only person in this unique act who understands and takes on our suffering, pain and death. The prophet Isaiah tells us:

*Surely, he took up our pain and bore our suffering.*
*He was pierced for our transgressions, he was crushed for our iniquities;*
*the punishment that brought us peace was on him, and by his wounds we*
*are healed. The Lord has laid on him the iniquity[132] of us all[133]*

I have allowed that balance to be tipped to one side, particularly in the last few years of licensed priestly ministry. On reflection, my desire to be compassionate developed, in some cases into wanting to be the person who sorted others' lives, eventually to the cost of my own health, and not being present enough for my wife and children. Exploring this through counselling, I was diagnosed with compassion fatigue which was another element in my mental breakdown. The main aspects of physical and emotional exhaustion are present in compassion fatigue, which is sometimes also called vicarious traumatisation. Like so many things, I did not do that consciously, but allowed it to develop within me. More about this in the chapter 'Out of your mind'.

In Matthew's Gospel, he recalls the occasion when Jesus feeds the five thousand. He writes:

*Jesus called his disciples to him and said, 'I have compassion for these people; they have already been with me three days and have nothing to eat. I do not want to send them away hungry, or they may faint on the way.' The disciples said to him 'Where are we to get enough bread in the desert to feed so great a crowd?'[134]*

Jesus replies to the disciples, enquiring to what they have available. They tell him that they have seven loaves and a few fish. In some accounts this is the feeding of the five thousand and a young boy comes forward with seven loaves and two fish. After asking the crowd to sit down, he takes what little food is available and performs a miracle, providing enough food for everyone. He hands it to the disciples, who distribute it and also clear up afterwards, collecting any scraps which are left.

This story of compassion leads to practical care – hunger satisfied by food. Jesus does not do everything, but rather it is a shared task. Jesus takes food, blesses it, breaks the bread and shares all the food available. Enough for everyone. It reminds me of the words on a card that was given to me at the ordination of being a priest:

*You are to be taken, blessed, broken, shared.*
*That the work of the incarnation[135] may go forward*

116

These are the actions of compassion that Jesus shows, but also the very heart of Jesus' life – for he was taken by God, blessed by him, broken by the world so that he might be shared in the lives of everyone. Those key words are so important for me, for they summarise my own calling by God, but equally are the invitation for us all. It is when we surrender our lives in this way that we allow God to be fully incarnate in us for the world to know and see. Henri Nouwen says:

> God, through Jesus, has made our bodies sacred places where God has chosen to dwell. Our faith in the resurrection of the body, therefore, calls us to care for our own and one another's bodies with love. When we bind one another's wounds and work for the healing of one another's bodies, we witness to the sacredness of the human body, a body destined for eternal life. [136]

The act of compassion and pastoral care is for everyone to live out. Having been a 'professional' in pastoral care for twenty years as licensed priest, I think the most frustrating thing is that the majority of people expect the priest to do all the pastoral care. 'Why hasn't the vicar been to visit me?' is a very well-used question. First of all, that is never practical concerning workload, but second, is not the model of the early church. Jesus brings together the twelve disciples, but later commissions seventy-two others, and then elders are commissioned, particularly for pastoral care. [137] The task of caring is for all. Admittedly, some people are more able and gifted to do this, and they should be encouraged. In some institutionally structured churches, elders and pastoral visitors/assistants are commissioned to do the task, thereby acting on behalf of the church. Church leaders who 'do' all the caring themselves deny the opportunity for those gifted to do it, but equally church leaders who do not do any pastoral caring are shirking on the responsibility given to them at their induction/licensing.

By using the word pastoral, I am meaning that care is to be holistic – care of body, mind and spirit. The phrase 'pastoral care' was used mostly by faith organisations, but in recent years is used by organisations of faith and no faith. It is present in well-run businesses and I am aware of some local family-run businesses who are excellent at taking care of their employees, one of which continues the task even after they have left the company's employment.

Being selective about who we are compassionate and care for is not acceptable. Tempting, but definitely not right. We must not withhold care for someone just because we don't like them, or we don't approve of what they say or might have done, or any other prejudice. Love in action by caring is not based on human judgement, but responding to the unconditional love God has for us – and all people. Don't allow the old expression 'Don't mind me', used sarcastically by those who believe that we have forgotten them or choose to ignore them. For those in leadership roles, in whatever context, I offer the words of Steven Knight, who recently adapted Charles Dickens' *A Christmas Carol*[138]. He says:

> *Dickens' point was that power without compassion is dangerous and lethal*
> ...

Leaders also need to be cared for with compassion in the way in which leaders care compassionately for those they lead. Teresa of Avila's 16th century prayer reminds us:

> *Christ has no body but yours,*
> *No hands, no feet on earth but yours,*
> *Yours are the eyes with which he looks*
> *With compassion on this world,*
> *Yours are the feet with which he walks to do good,*
> *Yours are the hands, with which he blesses all the world.*

# Out Of Your Mind
## Mental health

Being one with the mind of Christ is key for our health and wellbeing, but what about times when our mind is not in good health? When we are not thinking in a well-balanced way, it often leads to our actions not being in tune with our usual behaviour. Things that we might say or do are not 'normal'. This often leads to people saying 'are you out of your mind?', or even 'are you crazy?' Our mind is also out of sync with the mind of Christ. Even some people who at one point were around Jesus, said of him, 'He is out of his mind.'[139] It wasn't necessarily true, but they thought his behaviour was out of the normal.

I have always been aware and sympathetic of people with mental health issues. They can be in a vast range of different ways. I have been trained often on different aspects of mental health, which served me well as a parish priest and especially when overseeing pastoral care of a major youth project. I have sat in church porches with young people self-harming and standing with a young person whilst they cut their arm with a razor blade, and blood flowed onto the church altar cloths. I therefore have great respect for those who have poor mental health and also those who work with them. However, it is nothing compared to actually encountering it for yourself, and that is exactly what happened to me.

What I am about to say is as open and honest as I can possibly be. There may be things that will be highly critical and I cannot apologise for that because the facts and associated emotional feelings are absolutely true. This is entirely my encounter, as well as for several people alongside me at the time. It is therefore unique and other people's stories will be their own too.

One August afternoon I found myself being arrested and spent several hours in a police cell until I was processed and interviewed in the middle of the night. Being released in the early hours of the following morning I was returned home where I remember sitting up in bed, next to Pauline, my wife, and asking her 'What's happening to me?' She asked me why I hadn't talked to her about how I had been feeling. I simply couldn't do that because I thought that if I did, then she would not love me and our marriage would be over. I loved her too much to risk that possibility. The reality was that she loved me whatever, and there was part of me that knew that to be true, but I simply wasn't thinking straight. I remember feeling so numb, I think because of shock and not understanding how I had got myself in such a mess. Pauline immediately arranged for me to see a counsellor and within a few days I had my first session. Little did I realise that I would see them for almost two years and nearly eighty sessions. Attempting to understand what had happened took a lot of time and emotional energy, and what seemed like my whole life was unpacked and laid bare to help me understand myself and why I behaved in certain ways. There was no doubt that it was an enormous help despite feeling highly vulnerable.

My doctor was very supportive and also referred me to see a highly respected and experienced psychiatrist. After listening to me talk in my first session with him, he diagnosed me as suffering from burnout. He explained what that meant, telling me that the word 'burnout' comes from the rocket. When a rocket uses up its fuel, it still continues to travel. Observing it, you would not know anything was wrong, yet the rocket has burned out. Its travel is likely to be slower, but it will eventually get to a different destination than originally intended. He explained to me that is why I didn't know anything was really wrong and people around me, observing me, would not see anything very different to normal. I know that I cried when he finished talking to me, as well as when I recalled this to other people. There was something so important about having a diagnosis which meant that I had a platform to begin recovery. I didn't realise that it would take as long as it did – almost four years. I answered many of his questions as he enquired about my feelings, activities etc. over the previous few years. Apart from burnout, he diagnosed me with a depersonalisation disorder. It is where someone feels detached from their own identity and have no real control of their feelings and actions. For me, I felt as though I was living my life in a bubble, at times like a cotton wool bubble. I was getting on with my life, but things and people felt detached. I was increasingly struggling with relationships and, as in the rocket, I was taking longer to achieve tasks. When a few people heard my diagnosis, I am aware that they said 'Once he's rested and had a holiday, he will feel better in a few weeks.' That lack of understanding is that perhaps we tend to use the word burnout when we feel a bit more than tired or worn out. But believe me, true burnout is about having a mental breakdown, which, as I said, has taken me about four years to recover from. I suspect the trauma of the arrest and court case, plus the added trauma of the way my employers dealt with me, made the illness far worse.

Having my wife, family, close friends and professionals to support me has been invaluable. For some, their support came by personal sacrificial action. I am truly humbled and grateful that the mind of Christ was active in them. The Church of England paid for my counselling and psychiatrist sessions and also arranged for me to see a pastoral bishop. I am really grateful for that, but as I will explain later, the institution caused a great deal of stress and anxiety by their actions. Talking principally with those professionals, as well as Pauline, helped me to understand what had been happening and starting me on my journey to healing recovery.

The underlying issue which caused my mental breakdown was stress. Not just the short-term stress which we all encounter in everyday life[140], but excessive stress[141]. Stress influences how the brain is wired, making us extra-susceptible to future problems by destroying the very brain pathways that would help us to stay calm and in control. The more stress, the more brain pathways that are destroyed, meaning that we are less in control as stress builds. Psychologists including Greg Miller[142] say research suggests that stress in early life doesn't just make people vigilant for threat. It also affects reward circuits in the brain that regulate our appetites for everything from food to drugs, sex and money. As we know, body, mind and spirit are interconnected and so stress will be affecting the whole of our being. Catherine Loveday in her book on the brain says:

*Levels of cortisol increase when we wake up in the morning, driving our body to be ready for the demands of the day ahead ... That first waking increase in cortisol – the Cortisol Awaking Response – has been found to be a very significant indicator of health and wellbeing, and is often abnormal in people with type 2 diabetes, chronic fatigue syndrome, multiple sclerosis, burnout, amnesia, depression, eating disorders and PTSD (post-traumatic stress disorder), to name but a few.* [143]

My natural type is an introvert. A plus point for this is that when I am mentally well, I am naturally a person who reflects about what is going on, often before speaking. I am definitely not the 'life and soul of the party', preferring to spend leisure time with people I know and avoiding small-talk as much as I can. Quite a number of priests are introverts and I know find small-talk stressful. It is part of having to be an actor, functioning behind a mask of who people expect you to be, and do. Extroverts, are of course, the opposite of all this. For me, dealing with increased stress and having almost no time for myself meant that I was using small places to go to, knowing that people did not know where I was, and being free from demands and expectations. This desire developed, as my mental health deteriorated, into actions which were illegal, unacceptable and damaging for everyone. I was, and am, truly sorry for that, and the hurt it caused, and publicly wrote an apology in an open letter. The need for small spaces rises from my childhood. My mother was a compulsive cleaner and as a child I was expected to always be tidy, especially my bedroom. I used to build dens in the large garden – a space where I could do what I wanted, as well as play with my friends, without being constantly told to tidy up.

During my sessions with the psychiatrist, he told me that there was one important thing that I needed to do, and continue doing, from then on. He said, 'Martin, you need to take control.' I had to acknowledge that I operated with no boundaries and my life was controlled by those around me, rather than being responsible for myself, my wellbeing and work-life balance. I discussed this with my pastoral bishop, who I am deeply grateful for, as he listened with respect and patience, and responded with great experience, wisdom and the mind of Christ. Being a trained theologian[144], I needed someone to reflect with theologically, about all that had happened. Part of having no boundaries was that I became set in thinking that God required me to be sacrificial in priestly ministry. I needed to be available to whomever, at whenever and wherever. I was obsessed with God being in control and it took some time to understand that God shares that control with me, often in basic common sense and out of loving self, because we are worth it.

When my counsellor told me that I had a lack of self-worth, I was shocked. This had only developed in the last four years as a priest and linked to my lack of control and boundaries. My constant desire to help others didn't acknowledge that I too was worth taking good care of. This was something that seemed to deepen unconsciously and reflecting back, there were few times when people had given me praise. I can recall being at a clergy conference and in the evening sitting in the bar, listening to a colleague who had recently been appointed an archdeacon. He shared with us his disappointment and dismay that his church had not thanked him for what he had done at the annual meeting. I never really thought about it, but just presumed he wasn't doing a good job – until the same thing happened to me. In my last few years in post, I too was not thanked at the annual meeting. Considering this was the event when clergy thank everyone, usually by name and what they have done, I would have been in trouble if anyone had been left out! I even heard, on one occasion, someone in a leadership role say to someone that they didn't tell me what a good job I was doing because I might get a big head. Considering this was the largest of three churches I was currently leading, I am grateful that the others didn't forget me, as well as the previous ten churches that I had been involved with over the previous thirteen years. The current large church seemed increasingly to behave in a manner which expected me to do everything that a priest should do, because I was deemed to be the professional who was paid to do it all. Working with three churches to be collaborative was challenging at times, but I managed to form a large ministry team who were empowered to use and celebrate their gifts, and work together. Thank you to all of those who were part of that – a great amount was achieved and many in the team were volunteers. This collaborative approach was modelled by Jesus, as he called his disciples, then sent out another seventy-two people, and in the Book of Acts we read that elders were appointed for pastoral work so that others could concentrate on preaching. Enabling people's gifts is powerful rather than expecting everyone to be good at everything.

Early on in my counselling sessions, I was asked to go home and write down all the areas that were giving me stress. It took a full afternoon to type and filled six pages of A4 paper. I went to bed immediately after finishing – I was shaking, had a headache and felt awful. I think I stayed in bed a couple of full days finding it impossible to get up and probably suffering from aspects of depression. Talking the document through in my next session made me realise how bad things had become and I clearly was not handling life at all well. The counsellor said that one page of what I had written was bad for my health, let alone the events of six pages. Whilst I have always been an advocate of shared and collaborative ministry, I must confess that there were many times where I was a control freak. Being a perfectionist has always been a good and bad thing for me. Whatever I do has to be done to the absolute best it can be – that's good, however, not managed well it compounded my stress level and as that increased, I felt that I was on a never-ending circle of work, and not able to get off (clearly in hindsight the development of burnout). Having to realise that I had to take my part of the responsibility of getting into such poor mental health was sobering and important, so that I could take serious steps to ensure that it never happened again. The document that I had written covered the stresses of living in a very large house and garden with the oldest part of it suffering from water damage. Administration and some other aspects of the youth project had to be relocated with difficulty whilst the repairs took over two years to be started.

Due to changing culture and much more, the Church of England desperately needs to reimagine what church is, what it means, and how it is structured. More about that in a separate chapter, but as rural dean (a.k.a. an area manager!) I was heading up a wide consultation to formulate creative plans for the way twenty-two churches would work together. Following three years of careful work with my clergy colleagues and meetings with representatives of all the churches, I made a presentation of plans in one gathering of all the twenty-two church councils. One particular small group of churches was clearly angry about the plans and two people voiced their concerns in an abrasive manner during the question-and-answer session at the end. With a desire to meet them separately to listen and reply in person, I approached them after the meeting. Other people were still around but as I started in the conversation it immediately lapsed into two people giving me personal verbal abuse and making serious accusations which were absolutely not true. As I felt my fists clench, I at least reacted by immediately walking away. For me, this was clearly happening at the time of my burnout accelerating and this was part of 'the final straw'. I remember sending an email to two of my senior colleagues who simply replied with an 'oh dear' response. None of my clergy colleagues, at any level, made any attempt to help specifically address the inappropriate behaviour of the two people. After that meeting I know that overnight it was one of a few times when I was considering taking my own life. I don't think I ever got to the reality of actually planning to do so, but the thoughts were there, I suspect as this was a possible way out of how I had been feeling.

Apart from the stresses I have mentioned above, there were also aspects of finance; reordering the inside of church buildings (one of them especially a huge project); compassion fatigue (the build-up of the constant need to respond pastorally, seemed a never-ending task and became tiring); finding myself needing to avoid a very few people who were attention seekers; working with at least four colleagues who were demanding, mostly because of what had, and was going on in their own lives; what seemed like an increasing amount of 'red tape' to enable changes to take place; conflict with those who cannot cope with change; and much more too.

Pauline became increasingly aware that I was not coping and she offered to finish working in her private practice so that she could help me. She informed those with leading roles in the three churches, plus my immediate senior colleagues, to let them know that I was not coping. No tangible action followed and no immediate contact was made with me/us to listen to what was happening and how they could help. Amazingly, the week of my arrest was the time when Pauline finished her paid work. Literally, thank God, as without her I would never have been able to work through all that I have written about in this book.

There has been a great deal of research over the decades about clergy stress. Overall, research will tell us that being a priest is one of the most fulfilling jobs, for which I would personally agree wholeheartedly – until you are seriously stressed. Rayburn, Richmond and Roger, in their studies of 1986 on stress report

*Clergy stress occurs because of work overload, (too many meetings to the detriment of pastoral work, time pressures); role conflicts (balancing family and work priorities, conflicts between planned and crisis work, church conservation; role ambiguity ...; dealing with grief and people in need...); relationships with parishioners and parish (unrealistic demands ...); and self-pressures (inability to say no, not appreciating one's own limitations and difficulties in delegating).*

The greatest problem with the institutional church is that it consults and carries out research and publishes reports and has debate, but not much has actually been done to reduce stress – I suspect because the real way to do that is a massive rethink of its purpose and structures. Having more and more churches for one person to lead and oversee is for ever increasing, and will continue to do so.

The increasing stress and my deteriorating mental health affected my family life behind closed doors. I was drinking a bottle of red wine each night as well as added beer and spirits at the weekend. My sex drive was non-existent, I was short tempered, sometimes banging the table, banging doors and stomping off. Sleep patterns were disrupted and the feeling of self-isolation was compounded by the developing depersonalisation disorder. Sometimes I would lead an early Sunday morning service nursing a hangover headache, and I am aware that I was stumbling over words, and beginning to forget things.

Apart from the extreme stress, I then experienced all that came with my arrest and the additional trauma of the way that the Church of England dealt with the situation, me and my family. Whilst I have been very grateful for the financial funding for my mental health professionals, and conversations with a retired bishop, that is where the positive support ends. I had already spoken to a few colleagues who, whilst also acting illegally or inappropriately, said how disgusted they had been with the way the institutional church dealt with them. Their experience is not for me to share in detail, but I will share mine. The reason for doing so is to continue the honesty of experiences and because the desire is that changes might be made. I have little trust that will happen and more lives of leaders will attempt to be destroyed.

Over the period of a year, whilst I was rightly suspended from duties pending a court case and separate disciplinary proceedings, the local organisation of the Church of England (known as the diocese) committed several illegal breaches of civil law and ecclesiastical law against me. Bishops actively attempted to move me out of my house under the pretext of this being for our safety. When I refused to go, the action became so appalling that we had to source a specialist ecclesiastical solicitor to deal with this and other issues, in addition to the separate team for my legal case. Whilst suspended, I was still in post and legally 'owned' the house I was living in. Our solicitor was appalled at the way we were being treated (as well as our barrister) – actions which increased my stress level, added trauma and gave me depression, which needed medical treatment. What had happened to me was bad enough, let alone cruel treatment in this way that also stressed out my wife and three children. I was also accused of telling lies and being in places which I should not have been. Thankfully, and gratefully, this was all disproved and retracted, but only many weeks after. There was an instruction to the three church communities that they were not to make contact with us, which many seemed to carry out. Some did not do that and made contact, but they were met with cutting criticism and were accused of supporting my actions. This was absolutely not the case: the mind of Christ is to love the wrongdoer and hate the action that was committed (often described as 'hate the sin; love the sinner'). No one, and especially myself, has ever endorsed my inappropriate and illegal actions. When our solicitor challenged this, he was told that it was not true. This and other lies propagated were instrumental in a few close church friends severing their relationship with us. Some people walked on the other side of the road if they saw Pauline and me approaching. Many non-churchgoers commented to us that they were appalled by what church members were saying about me, and that was partly why they saw the church as hypocritical. I am deeply saddened that from our experience I must agree. Jesus speaks of a story about a person who is in need, lying in the road. Many people see the person but walk by on the opposite side of the road (this includes a priest). It is only a Samaritan who stops, attends the man and goes the extra mile to provide hospitality. Our experience is so similar: the institution passed by on the opposite side. Thank God for those people of faith, and those declaring no faith, who scooped us up, loved us and supported us. Some senior church leaders have said that on top of my illness and actions that I have also been a victim in this context. Whilst saying this, my bishop did meet informally with my wife and I on two occasions. In the final session he gave an emotional and genuine apology for his 'lack of duty of care'. We were both appreciative of that. Thank you.

Finding written accounts of church leaders who have experienced stress, burnout and therefore often mental breakdown is rare to find. Maybe this is because it is such a devastating personal and public event that it takes serious energy – emotional and physical, to recount what has happened. I know for myself that particularly this chapter has been like 'wading through treacle' to put into words. The spiritual battle to finally get here has been huge. However, I did find a book by R Loren Sandford called *Renewal for the Wounded Warrior – A burnout survival guide for believers*. It was so helpful to read someone else's account of burnout as a church leader which had such similarity to my own. This was especially valuable during the times when I felt I was the only one. His experience of how the Christian Church dealt with him seems, sadly, to mirror mine, as he writes:

> *Frequently, inner pressures of hurt and despair combine with the continuing demands of day-to-day life, labour or ministry to produce a devastating breakdown. Rather than respond with restorative compassion, the body of Christ too often beats the wounded one to death with religious platitudes and backstabbing suspicions. Years ago, a friend of mine said that the body of Christ is the only army in the world that shoots its wounded. How true!*[145]

Finishing this chapter on a positive note, my wife, children and family are so grateful for over 120 cards and letters, plus texts and messages and small gifts. Some came from people who didn't come to any of the churches, but part of the wider community, and some I had only met once or twice. Receiving texts and emails with prayers from people, including members of the youth project, wanting to know how I was, saying that I had been there for them in tough times and they now wanted to be there for me. Prayers were sent or sentences from messages I had sent to others saying, 'You sent this to me when I needed it, now I am sending it to you.' Those were deeply moving and emotional times. Thank you.

You may be wondering why I have not mentioned God very much in what I have written so far. God has been awesomely faithful and good to me and those around me. Yes, it has been tough and difficult, but what has developed through it has strengthened Pauline and my relationship with God. God has very clearly worked through so many people for his love, care, forgiveness and strength to be so tangible. I have written elsewhere about the blessings we wrote down each day over the period of ten months. They are precious memories and written down to remind us. Counterbalancing the way the institutional church acted, I am so grateful for those I came into contact with from the local police and probation service. Their pastoral care and respect for me was outstanding, especially when a diocesan representative said something private and inappropriate on local radio. The local press picked this up immediately and the police and probation service made immediate contact to see if I was ok. No apology from the church, or pastoral care concerning this issue was made.

It is good to know that the World Health Organisation has now recognised burnout as a serious issue, describing it as a 'syndrome conceptualised as resulting from chronic workplace stress that has not been successfully managed'. A local doctor wrote, 'Understanding and compassion are key to the recovery of someone with a mental illness. Not blame, not reprimand. Not told they're weak. Let's not forget that one day, it could be us.'[146] I can only hope and pray that the institutional church, and the legal system, makes an effort to understand mental health issues, by speaking to those who have encountered them, and treating them and their experience with value and respect. At the moment we are a very long way from that.

# A Goal In Mind
## The church

The majority of my life has been as part of the institutional church. Beginning at the age of six when I was recruited to join the church choir, then around fifteen years old I left to be an assistant Sunday school leader, followed by leading young people's groups of all ages. As my teen years came to a close, I helped to set up a young adult's group as well as being a member of the Parochial Church Council. After Pauline and I married, we moved to a church nearer our new home, becoming involved in young people's work, leading homegroups, church governance, building projects, healing and prayer ministry. The major change came when I was selected, trained and ordained as an Anglican priest.

Over the first 18 years of my life, I was mainly part of churches in Ipswich which had a choral and evangelical tradition. When I met my wife, Pauline, we would attend the Anglican Church that I was based at on Sunday mornings and then both attend Pauline's church, which was Baptist, in the evenings. My three years as a curate was based at an Anglo-Catholic church with Evangelical preaching and Charismatic worship (a fabulous combination!). Afterwards I worked within a team leading three very different churches in Bury St Edmunds where we were part of one church within the context of a needy housing estate (almost an urban priority area). When I became a full-time priest, I took on six rural churches newly put together, enabling them to work together and we saw the congregation size triple, and in some more than that. Then on to three churches; one in the large market town with two others close by in small villages. Across that time, I gained great experience of urban and rural churches and those with Anglo-Catholic, Evangelical, central and 'no-label' styles. Over twenty years as a priest, my ministry has been largely focused on enabling change, healing and prayer ministry, collaborative ministry and a large youth project. Across my lifetime I have gained a great deal of knowledge and experience of being part of the institutional Christian Church and I am deeply grateful for that time. I have had the enormous privilege of being alongside people at every aspect of life, seen people come to faith in God, enabled change in countless ways, started and overseen building development and fabric maintenance projects, shared my knowledge and experience of faith and scripture and been part of some amazing communities. The solitary member of clergy who wrote to me and told me that my ministry had been a failure is not correct – the success is about a faithful God working through me, whose desire was to be as faithful to my calling as I could humanly be. It seems important to share all of the above because of what I am about to say in the rest of this chapter.

Whilst as a licensed parish priest I have worked alongside and led thirteen churches. All of those church communities acknowledge that the church needs to change. Some have dared to be more radical than others, particularly five of them. The reason for change is that the number of people attending churches has declined, and continues to decline rapidly.

The weekly church attendance for Anglican churches in 2009 was 1,082,000. In 2018 that declined to 870,000. That is around a 23 per cent fall.[147] In 2038, if the fall is constant (and I suspect it will increase), then in the space of thirty years the number of people attending church regularly will have declined by around 50 per cent. It does not take too much maths to calculate how many years before the church building may be empty! The Why Church organisation[148] commented about this decline in this way:

*If the Church in England was the national football team, we would have sacked the manager long ago. A European social study (published in 2002) put the UK at the 4th lowest rate of church attendance in Europe.*

In 1983 two-thirds of the UK population went to church; in 2018 that declined to one-third. That decline is greater in some denominations: the Methodist Church (with 30.5 per cent decline); United Reformed Church (with 19 per cent decline in eight years); the Catholic Church (with 31 per cent decline); the Baptist Church (with 41 per cent decline in twenty years)[149]. Overall, the rate of decline in attendance is fairly consistent across the Christian faith. That decline also applies to those who offered, were selected, trained and ordained as priests/pastors/church leaders. This result is a reduced number of leaders caring for more church communities across the institutional church, but especially in the Church of England where there is often a church in every community and far more in urban areas. In my experience it is fascinating that, even armed with this information, there are people in churches who choose not to listen or simply don't care 'as long as you don't change anything that happens here.'

There are, of course, some churches which 'buck the trend' for a number of reasons: often because they are situated in towns and cities; have college/university communities; are financially wealthier; have outstanding leadership. The Archbishop of Canterbury, Justin Welby acknowledges 'that where you have a good vicar, you will find growing churches'[150]. Cathedral attendance has only reduced by 13 per cent in the last decade. In the last few years that has slowed as they report a stable Sunday attendance but a 35 per cent rise in midweek acts of worship. A close look at the statistics show that it is the main seasonal services (such as Christmas, Lent, Easter, Harvest etc.) that have increased, which has balanced the majority of Sundays small decline. My personal view is that there are those who travel to cathedrals because they prefer the formality; do not want to get involved with doing anything; don't like their local church/community. It's a bit like not wanting to shop locally but preferring to travel to a larger shopping centre for that experience, because travel makes this accessible.

A study in 2018[151] is very telling: When UK adult respondents were asked to select adjectives to define the church, 24 per cent chose 'Hypocritical', 23 per cent chose 'Judgemental', 9 per cent chose 'Relevant'. Those taking part were a mixture of church attendees and those who were not. Whilst I have been aware of this kind of response for many years, from my wife's and my own experience since 2016, I would agree wholeheartedly. There is a worrying reality that what the church community says and does can be vastly different from what it 'preaches'.

The United Reform Church, in its booklet entitled 'Missional Discipleship: What is it?'[152] opens with this paragraph:

*What we are seeing is a rapidly accelerating disconnection from institutional Christianity, coupled with widespread and growing active hostility towards the church. It is happening across all the mainstream denominations. This cannot be explained as a contemporary apathy towards faith, a general decline in moral standards or a lack of interest in spirituality. The problem is that people perceive and experience the Christian Church as Bad News.*

The disconnection from institutional Christianity is very real. Pauline and I have joined that disconnection, together with an increasing number of people who have made contact with us recently. The church increasingly does what it has always done, mainly in the way that it has always done it, and no longer helps people 'scratch where they itch'. One of my last churches has even said after my departure, 'Well, now we can get back to what we always did, and if people don't like it, they can go somewhere else' – and, of course, some have!

In some strong wings of the church there is an arrogance that 'we have the right answers to life's questions and we want you to come and listen to us tell you, and then, if you agree, you can join us.' This then leads to the subject of language ... don't get my started! I've written about this in the chapter headed *Mind your language* so forgive me, please, for repeating myself, but in my view this is so important and one of the reasons the institution is in rapid decline. It is abundantly clear that the majority of the population struggles with the language of the church. If you are 'in the club' (a member of church), and been so for some time, then you probably can understand (at some level) or cope with the language of most translations of the Bible and the liturgy used for church services. I am not suggesting that this needs to be taken away, but rather that additions are made. The organised church should be putting itself in the shoes of the person who is not 'in the club'. Putting up big posters which say 'Jesus is the Way, the Truth and the Life' is, quite frankly, pointless, and pushes people further away rather than to be inquisitive and enquire. The Bible sentence is true, but what we have ignored is that it is out of context of the whole message, and also completely impossible to understand to most people. The key, I believe, is always to do what Jesus did – meet people where they are (physically, culturally); speak to them in their own level of language; listen

133

carefully to what they are saying, because what they say is worth listening to and receiving; value and love them unconditionally; never judge; but always be true to what you believe, but open to what they believe. This needs to apply to every human being in every context. Long gone are the days when most children went to Sunday school and a large part of the population were forced or expected to go to church on Sunday. Most of the schools had acts of worship to begin each day, and would teach/study the Christian faith.

As a church leader I have observed and encountered the fact that is very clear that people have different levels of faith, experience and needs, and I have used this analogy often: there are those who are just beginning to explore faith (nursery school); those who want to commit by starting to live their faith for real (primary school); those who have some experience and beginning to form their own views and enjoy exploring more and developing a hunger for a meaningful relationship with God (secondary/high school); those taking leadership roles, read and study scripture, debate and have a longing for others to know God, perhaps as they do (university). Those doing a PhD and Masters are spiritually wise and have a deep knowledge and experience of God in their lives and the world. I've not used this grouping publicly, as people may feel inferior or judged. However, we do have to acknowledge that this faith journey exists. Some people progress along the route, some people choose, or for whatever reason, to stay at one particular part. Brian McLaren, in his excellent book called *The Great Spiritual Migration*, makes a similar point, naming it the Dance of Development and label each stage as God 0.1 through to God 0.5.[153] Whatever groupings or names that we might give them, the fact remains that members of the church are very different to each other in so many ways. Expecting that every week they will all come together to do the same thing, using the same language, is like putting everyone in university and wondering why people don't keep coming. In other words, not everyone has vast experience, knowledge and understanding of faith and academic ability as if they were accepted for the university of Christian faith.

Realising that the church is declining in numbers of people means that, particularly over the last twenty years, there have been vast numbers of projects generated to boost numbers. Yes, there will have been people who have responded to that approach, but it will not be many – certainly not to replace the number of people who have died or decided to leave. Many things have been 'pimped up', such as music, to become trendier and supposedly more appealing to young people. Every church that I have led asked me to bring in young people and young families, but when they came, they were glared at because they made a noise (the wrong sort of noise at the wrong time!) and often people never spoke to them because they were too consumed with their own clique during coffee after the service. No wonder they left and didn't come back. The problem is that all of these changes are simply 'rearranging chairs on the Titanic'. In other words, what the church thinks are major changes are still not enough to halt the decline in numbers, or more importantly to increase them.

There is absolutely no doubt that the institutional church realises that there is a serious and urgent problem. My experience is that it will not do what it says it should, which is to be radical. Their understanding of radical comes with baggage of the past and the obsession of keeping church buildings open and the structure of the institution in place. The Church of England declares that it is based on scripture, tradition and reason. The fascinating thing is that Jesus in scripture does not tell anyone to go to the temple every week. Rather, as we read in the Book of Acts, the church has a very simple model of a few people meeting together, and when they do so, Jesus asks that they share a meal and remember him and all that he has done for us. It is a church which is modelled on him – one who loves unconditionally and freely forgives. The URC booklet (quoted above) goes on later to say:

*The Church will not be renewed to look like Jesus until it recognises that it is addicted to survival. Survivalism is the greatest temptation for a church under pressure, and is the direct opposite of the process of the Way of the Cross. The salvation of Easter would not have been possible, had Jesus prioritised his own survival. A church in survival mode makes decisions based on prolonging its life. It asks. 'How can we use our resources to extend our life as long as possible?' rather than, 'How can we use our resources more effectively to make a Jesus-shaped difference to the lives of our people and communities?'*

135

Brian McLaren takes a similar view, as do I, when he writes in his book:

*Whenever I find myself in conversations about 'saving the church', I can't help but recall Jesus' words: 'if you want to save your life, you will lose it, but if you lose your life for my sake, you will find it.' Jesus' words make me wonder: could our desire to save our precious religious institutions and traditions actually hasten their demise? Could it be that the Spirit of God is calling the church to stop trying to save itself, and instead to join God in saving the world? Could pouring out itself for the good of the world be the only way for the church to save its own soul?[154]*

Having the mind of Christ in this is crucial. Discovering and having a goal in mind as to what church is all about is an essential building block. I suggest the starting point is studying the model of the early Church as set up by Jesus and his disciples. Dennis Kinlaw writes:

*I am convinced that every great revival in the history of the church has started when God's people began to seek the mind of Christ. When they set aside the normal human way of thinking about the world and allowed Christ to direct their lives, the world has been turned upside down.[155]*

I have always loved 'blue-sky thinking' — taking a blank sheet of paper and brainstorming creatively. The concept of church was set up by Jesus and is therefore important, but the way in which the church operates simply has to be appropriate for the time and culture we are in. We cannot constrain God when we ask him what church needs to be like now by telling him that anything goes, but not this, this, this and this. If we were doing it right and in accordance with what God desires at this time, then his church would be full — and it is absolutely not! We need to stop dragging people, kicking and screaming into our churches. Vincent Donovan, Catholic priest and missionary said:

*Do not try to call them back to where they were, and do not try to call them to where you are, as beautiful as that place might seem to you. You must have the courage to go with them to a place that neither of you, nor they have ever been before.*

What church is to be is something which is brand new – new for everyone. That is so exciting.

You may think that Martin Thrower has beaten the institutional church over the head with a big stick and the chapter is about to finish, and he hasn't said what the church should be like. Very true! That's the subject of another book, I think.

# Mind How You Go
## The way forward – be confident and let go!

The awesome reality is that each of us has access to the way that God thinks! The mind of Christ is the mind of God in human form and by the Holy Spirit enables us to access that mind. Saint Paul, writing to the Church in Corinth tells them (and therefore us too):

*... as it is written, 'What no eye has seen, nor ear heard, nor the human heart conceived, what God has prepared for those who love him'—*

*these things God has revealed to us through the Spirit; for the Spirit searches everything, even the depths of God. For what human being knows what is truly human except the human spirit that is within? So also no one comprehends what is truly God's except the Spirit of God. Now we have received not the spirit of the world, but the Spirit that is from God, so that we may understand the gifts bestowed on us by God. And we speak of these things in words not taught by human wisdom but taught by the Spirit, interpreting spiritual things to those who are spiritual.*

*Those who are unspiritual do not receive the gifts of God's Spirit, for they are foolishness to them, and they are unable to understand them because they are spiritually discerned. Those who are spiritual discern all things, and they are themselves subject to no one else's scrutiny. 'For who has known the mind of the Lord so as to instruct him?'*

*But we have the mind of Christ.*[156]

Having the mind of Christ is not a spiritual goal, it is what we have freely received from the One who created us.

138

The mind of Christ shows us the things God has freely given to us, with 'no holds barred'. Despite living in a broken world, being people who are sometimes broken, in body, mind and spirit, the reality is that God loves each of us beyond our human understanding, no matter who we are, no matter what we may have thought, said or done. God's love is never ending, always present and comes with forgiveness by the bucket load!

The mind of Christ means that we do not have to prove ourselves to God. He believes in us. He values us. We are incredibly special and important to him.

The mind of Christ is an opportunity to see God the Father as Jesus sees him, and how the fullness of God's love sees us.

The mind of Christ means that God is in us, always. There is nowhere and no time that the mind of Christ is not accessible.

It is difficult to convey in words the devastation and trauma I, my wife and family experienced during the darkest period of my life. I lost my job, we lost our home, and I ended up with a criminal conviction. There was a period of three weeks between my employment with the Church of England ending and being able to move into our little rental home. Despite a request, the church in Suffolk (known as the diocese), refused to allow us to stay for that short extra time. We found ourselves officially homeless. We were now the ones being taken in by friends, scooped up and given shelter, food, and emotional care, as we started the rebuilding of our lives. We experienced how impossible it is to get a home with a criminal conviction, despite having the money to pay rent. We needed a short-term housing option to take time to work out where we wanted to buy a home, and we are incredibly grateful to friends who made that possible. Trying to arrange car insurance was also a nightmare!

Apart from those around us who chose to support us with love and care, we were 'burned out in the embers of the fire'. Rejected by some, and worse still, by the institution that I had served God faithfully through, for the previous twenty years. I was well and truly 'knocked off the pedestal'!

However – through it all has been, and is, God. We had learned early on to look for where he was, as we wrote down our blessings. God was definitely present – blessing us every day. That process continues now as we rebuild our lives anew, making good use of the wisdom, through experiences in our life, individually and together, enabled by the mind of Christ.

I therefore speak with a great deal of experience to say confidently, that the mind of Christ enables our lives to be transformed. What appears to be lost, gone wrong, made a mess of and perhaps we feel failed, is part of the never-ending work of transformation that the Almighty God does supremely in our world and in our lives. As 'The Story of the Fire Lily' reminds us:

*And from the ashes of our lives*
*God resurrects us, too.*

It is essential that we remind ourselves often that *all* things are possible with God. We are in partnership with him, a partnership of love that flourishes when we trust in him. That trust is about a great deal of letting go to God:

Letting go our regrets about the past.
Letting go our anxiety about the future and the choices we face at this moment.
Letting go what hurts and our resentment.
Letting go of our need to be good enough.
Letting go of our desire for growth.
Letting God be God!

Hard as it may seem, and actually often is, letting God be God in our lives is what he longs for – not that we should be chess pieces, moved around on the game of life, but rather because we are in partnership with him. That really is the overarching aspect of my life, and my married life with Pauline. God has been, is, and will continue to be faithful, particularly when we let go of all that holds us back from being transformed people full of potential.

All of this is made possible through the birth, life, death and resurrection of Jesus Christ. That is why we can be confident. Thank God, I say!

*In Christ alone my hope is found*
*He is my light, my strength, my song*
*This Cornerstone, this solid ground*
*Firm through the fiercest drought and storm*
*What heights of love, what depths of peace*
*When fears are stilled, when strivings cease*
*My Comforter, my All in All*
*Here in the love of Christ I stand*

*In Christ alone, who took on flesh*
*Fullness of God in helpless babe*
*This gift of love and righteousness*
*Scorned by the ones He came to save*
*'Till on that cross as Jesus died*
*The wrath of God was satisfied*
*For every sin on Him was laid*
*Here in the death of Christ I live*

*There in the ground His body lay*
*Light of the world by darkness slain*
*Then bursting forth in glorious Day*
*Up from the grave He rose again*
*And as He stands in victory*
*Sin's curse has lost its grip on me*
*For I am His and He is mine*
*Bought with the precious blood of Christ*

*No guilt in life, no fear in death*
*This is the power of Christ in me*
*From life's first cry to final breath*
*Jesus commands my destiny*
*No power of hell, no scheme of man*
*Can ever pluck me from His hand*
*'Till He returns or calls me home*
*Here in the power of Christ I'll stand*[157]

# MIND HOW YOU GO!

Go into the world
God is there before you
Christ fought and conquered there
Eternity has broken into time,
And the future is secure.
The blessing of God Almighty, Father, Son & Holy Spirit
Be with you, and with all people
Now and always. Amen

# Bibliography

Joyce Meyer *Battlefield of the Mind – Winning the Battle of Your Mind* (Hodder, Edition 2008)

Justin Welby *Dethroning Mammon – Making Money Serve Grace* (Bloomsbury 2016)

Henri Nouwen *In the name of Jesus* (DLT 2000)

Dennis F Kinlaw *The Mind of Christ* (Francis Asbury Press 1998)

Bill Johnson *The Supernatural Power of a Transformed Mind* (Destiny Image 2005)

Alan Smith & Peter Shaw *The Reflective Leader* (Canterbury Press 2011)

Jo Marchant *Cure – A Journey into the Science of Mind over Body* (Canongate 2017)

Michel Quoist *Prayers of Life* (Logos Books 1965)

Catherine Loveday *The Secret World of the Brain* (Sevenoaks 2017)

Rowan Williams *The Wound of Knowledge* (DLT 1979)

Yvonne Warren *The Cracked Pot – The State of Today's Anglican Parish Clergy* (Kevin Mayhew 2002)

R Loren Sandford *Renewal for the Wounded Warrior. A burnout survival guide for believers* (New Song Church and Ministries 2010)

Paul Gilbert & Coden *Mindful Compassion* (Constable & Robinson 2013)

Rowan Williams *Open to Judgement* (DLT 1994 & 2014)

Henri J M Nouwen *The Return of the Prodigal Son. A story of homecoming* (DLT 1994)

Philip Yancy *Whats so Amazing about Grace?'* (Zondervan 1997)

W H Vanstone *The Stature of Waiting* (DLT 1982)

Carlo Carretto *Letters from the Dessert* (DLT 1972)

Henri Nouwen *In the name of Jesus* (DLT 2000)

Pete Greig *God on Mute* (David C Cook, Kingsway Communications 2007)

Ruby Wax *Frazzled* (Penguin Life 2016)

John O'Donohue *Benedictus – A Book of Blessings* (Transworld 2007)

Jean-Pierre de Caussade *The Sacrament of the Present Moment* (Harper Collins 1966 & 1989)

Brian D McLaren *The Great Spiritual Migration* (Hodder 2016)

# Notes

1    John 1: 1-2
2    John 1: 3
3    Genesis 1:1-2
4    Colossians 1: 27-28
5    1 Corinthians 2: 16
6    Philippians 2: 4-5
7    John 14: 12
8    D F Kinlaw – *The Mind of Christ*. p. 14
9    Matthew 5: 41
10   John 16: 1-15
11   Philippians 2: 5-8
12   Luke 9: 23
13   Luke 12: 48b
14   The Oxford Movement was a movement of High Church members of the Church of England which eventually developed into Anglo-Catholicism.
15   James 1: 17 (New King James version)
16   Luke 18: 19 (New King James version)
17   Lyrics by Don Moen
18   A phrase meaning bad things start to happen.
19   Genesis 3: 1
20   This part of the story of Genesis is often called 'The Fall'.
21   Genesis 3: 13-24
22   More names include the accuser, the evil one, the tempter, Beelzebub.
23   Revelation 12
24   2 Peter 2: 4
25   Matthew 25:41
26   Job 1: 8-12 (The Message Bible)
27   Those who lived out of Palestine, or who were scattered among the Gentiles.
28   James 1: 13
29   1 Peter 5:8-9

[30] A short act of reflective worship forming part of the Divine Office of the Western Christian Church, traditionally said (or chanted) before retiring for the night.

[31] Matthew 16: 24

[32] Ephesians 6: 12-13

[33] Luke 4: 1-13

[34] Luke chapter 10

[35] Luke 10: 17-20 (New King James version)

[36] James 1: 2-4 (The Message Bible)

[37] Quote by Lisa Bever

[38] Words by Johnson Oatman (1897)

[39] Romans 8: 38-39

[40] Romans 3: 23

[41] John 13: 34

[42] Mark 12: 29-31

[43] Romans 7: 21-8:14 (The Message Bible)

[44] John 8:7

[45] Matthew 7:3

[46] James 1: 14-15

[47] Revelation 21

[48] Staff writer, desiring God.org

[49] Words by Percy Dreamer MA (1925)

[50] Henri J M Nouwen – *The Return of the Prodigal Son* p. 82

[51] Luke 15: 11-32

[52] Henri J M Nouwen – *The Return of the Prodigal Son* p. 13

[53] © Martin Thrower

[54] Exodus 20: 2-17

[55] Matthew 22: 37-39

[56] John 4: 19-21 (The Message Bible)

[57] Philip Yancy – *What's so Amazing about Grace*

[58] Justin Welby – *Dethroning Mammon* p. 84

[59] Luke 6: 36

[60] Thomas Merton. Trappist Monk. (1915–1968)

[61] The Big Issue. 16–26 December 2019 p. 21

[62] Author unknown

[63] The Message Bible

[64] Genesis 1: 1-4

[65] Genesis 2: 1

66 Genesis 2: 5-7 & 15
67 Genesis 2: 18-22
68 The name NOOMA comes from a phonetic spelling of the Greek word pneuma, meaning 'wind', 'spirit', or 'breath'.
69 Church of England: Common Worship. Eucharistic Prayer G
70 Athenians – custodians of teachings, met here at the hill of Ares.
71 From the Cretan poet Epimenides c. 600BC.
72 Acts 17: 24-28
73 Joyce Meyer Battlefield of the Mind p.16
74 Marianne Williamson. Often miscredited to Nelson Mandela.
75 More on Ignatian Spirituality at www.ignatianspitituality.com.
76 Ronald Stuart Thomas (1913–2000) Welsh poet & Anglican Priest.
77 2 Timothy 3: 16
78 A person who seeks by contemplation and self-surrender to obtain unity with God, believing in the spiritual apprehension of truths that are beyond the intellect.
79 First two verses only. © David J Evans
80 Carlo Carretto (1910–1988. Italian writer, Catholic mystic) Letters from the Dessert pp. 55-56
81 Pete Greig God on Mute Engaging the silence of unanswered prayer.
82 www.retreats.og.uk
83 Mark 6: 30-32
84 Henri Nouwen In the Name of Jesus p. 30
85 Genesis 2: 18-24
86 Also known as 'call to priesthood'
87 www.spidir.org.uk
88 The Sacrament of the Present Moment by Jean-Pierre de Caussade
89 'Frazzled' by Ruby Wax
90 1 Samuel 3: 9 (The Message Bible)
91 www.dictionary.com
92 www.dictionary.com
93 Matthew 18: 15-20 (The Message Bible)
94 Philippians 2: 1-9
95 'The Cracked Pot' page 206
96 John O'Donohue 'Benedictus' A Book of Blessings
97 21st Century King James Bible © 1994 Denel Enterprises Inc
98 Sir Francis Drake (1540-1596)
99 1 Corinthians 15: 40, 44

[100] Revelation 21: 1-5 The Message Bible
[101] Genesis 15:1
[102] Genesis 46:2
[103] Acts 16:9
[104] Daniel 2: 28
[105] Matthew 14: 13-21
[106] French poet and philosopher who combined Christianity, socialism and patriotism.
[107] Advent – the season of waiting and preparation for Jesus birth (Christmas).
[108] Lent – the season of waiting and preparation for Jesus death and resurrection (Good Friday to Easter).
[109] Revelation 8: 1
[110] Mark 6: 30-44
[111] John Henry Newman (1801–1890) was an English theologian and poet, first an Anglican priest and later a Catholic priest and cardinal.
[112] Written between 29 & 19BC
[113] 1685-1753
[114] Theologist is someone trained theology: the nature of God in the world. 'Theo' being God as Father, Son and Holy Spirit.
[115] James 1: 17
[116] Malachi 3: 6
[117] Hebrews 13: 8
[118] St Cedd c 620–664. Anglo-Saxon monk and bishop from the Kingdom of Northumbria.
[119] Dennis F Kinlaw – The Mind of Christ p.33
[120] John 17: 13-19 (The Message Bible)
[121] Romans 12: 2 (New International version)
[122] Ref: John 15: 15
[123] Romans 8: 16-18
[124] Psalm 23: 3
[125] Jordan Peterson; psychologist and bestselling author. Item in The Sunday Times Magazine. Date unknown.
[126] Justin Welby Dethroning Mannon pp. 89-90
[127] John 4: 1-30
[128] Matthew 28: 18-20
[129] John 14: 11-14 (The Message Bible)
[130] From their book Mindful Compassion, introduction p. xx.
[131] Luke chapters 22 & 23

[132] Meaning the essence of our sin/our wrongdoing

[133] Isaiah 53: 4-6

[134] Matthew 15: 32-33

[135] God reveals himself as a human being in Jesus Christ. Jesus is fully human but equally fully God.

[136] Source unknown

[137] Acts 14 & 15

[138] Three-part adaptation for television. First shown December 2019..

[139] Mark 3: 21

[140] Known as good stress (eustress).

[141] Known as bad stress (distress).

[142] Professor at Weinberg College, Department of Psychology

[143] Catherine Loveday *The Secret World of the Brain* pp. 58-59

[144] Theologian, meaning to study and expound God in the world.

[145] p. xiv

[146] Dr Matt Piccaver. Suffolk Magazine December 2016

[147] Source: The Church of England

[148] Whychurch.org.uk

[149] Source of all statistics from the individual websites.

[150] In an interview with BBC Radio 4 Today Programme (Date unknown)

[151] The UK Church in Action study 2018.

[152] Booklet produced by The North Western Synod of the United Reformed Church, 2017 © Lawrence Moore, Walking the Walk Publications. See www.walkingthewalk.org.uk

[153] pp. 98–118

[154] p. 160

[155] Acts 17: 6. Dennis F Kinlaw, *The Mind of Christ* p. 19

[156] 1 Corinthians 2: 9-16

[157] Songwriters: Andrew Shawn Craig & Don Koch

9 781789 633382